Shakespeare
AND
THE
ENDS
OF
Comedy

Drama and Performance Studies

Timothy Wiles, General Editor

Ejner J. Jensen

Shakespeare and the Ends of Comedy

INDIANA UNIVERSITY PRESS
Bloomington and Indianapolis

The paper used in this publication meets the minimum requirements of American National Standard for Information Sciences—Permanence of Paper for Printed Library Materials, ANSI Z39.48-1984.

Manufactured in the United States of America

Library of Congress Cataloging-in-Publication Data

Jensen, Ejner J.
Shakespeare and the ends of comedy / Ejner J. Jensen.
p. cm. — (Drama and performance studies)
Includes bibliographical references (p.) and index.
ISBN 0-253-33094-7 (cloth)
1. Shakespeare, William, 1564–1616—Comedies. 2. Comedy.
I. Title. II. Series.
PR2981.J4 1991
822.3'3—dc20 90-23962

1 2 3 4 5 95 94 93 92 91

For Pozi

Contents

Acknowledgments

All writers acquire debts; those who write on Shakespeare acquire a more varied and extensive list of creditors than most others. In addition to the usual personal and professional obligations, a writer who ventures to discuss Shakespeare's plays also must acknowledge the importance of all those whose work in the theatre or on film or television has helped to illuminate the playwright's work. While I signal that acknowledgment only occasionally in the chapters that follow, I hope that in some way its reflection appears more or less steadily throughout this book.

Other debts are easier to be explicit about and no less pleasurable to record. John Knott helped to arrange the leave that allowed me to begin this work, and Bob Weisbuch was a welcome, even necessary, encouraging presence as I brought it to a close. To them, and to the University of Michigan for a sabbatical leave, I am deeply grateful. David DeLaura was a generous and thoughtful host at the University of Pennsylvania, extending me a courtesy appointment during my stay there; throughout that period, Georgianna Ziegler and her staff in the Furness Shakespeare Library made my days smooth and profitable.

Parts of the manuscript of this study benefited from early readings by David Bevington, Chris Hassel, and Marilyn Williamson; each of them encouraged me in a different fashion, while each of them gave me just the help I needed at the time. Charles Forker read the manuscript for the Indiana University Press and balanced sound advice with helpful approbation. Virginia Vaughan invited me to participate in the 1988 Shakespeare Association of America meeting in Boston on a topic quite different from the one addressed here and unwittingly gave this work a needed impetus; I remain thankful for that and for her friendship over many years.

Locally, Jill LeRoy-Frazier gave me research aid and indispensable computer assistance at a key moment. A more long-term debt is the one I owe to Linda Deitert for her unstinting and consistently cheerful help over the whole course of this book's preparation.

Some obligations, of course, are so personal and deep that they remain almost beyond the range of language and the ordinary expressions of thanks. What I owe to Sten and Maren belongs in this category. But an even deeper obligation is the one I have to my wife, who cared about this work and, in profoundly useful ways, cared for it from its inception to its completion. With thanks and affection, therefore, I dedicate it to her.

Introduction

This study of Shakespearean comedy grows out of the perception suggested by the deliberate ambiguity of its title: that modern criticism has confounded the endings of the comedies with the purposes of comedy. Another way of asserting the same point is to speak, as I do in the first chapter, of "The Aggrandizement of Closure." The study begins with an analysis of the modern criticism of Shakespearean comedy, dating from the publication of John Russell Brown's survey of the extant criticism in the mid-fifties. The development of criticism of the comedies since that time has been rapid and extensive, but it has been shaped by two dominant figures, Northrop Frye and C. L. Barber. While everyone recognizes the strength of their influence, no one has shown how their theories of comedy have concentrated critical attention on closure. The results of that concentration have been twofold. First, the aggrandizement of closure has transformed comedy, which is in its essence a matter of local effects and moment-to-moment theatrical pleasures, into a genre whose design and meaning are understood teleologically. Second, this stress on the interpretive primacy of closure has led to a critical situation in which contrary readings of the same play depend for their support on evidence drawn from the same material. Thus two critics who view *The Merchant of Venice* in opposed ways (one seeing it as moving toward final harmony, the other seeing it as discordant and problematic) derive their views from the identical materials. Those materials are essentially the closing moments of the play, and the critics have been influenced to seek meaning there by the dominant tradition of comic criticism, a tradition shaped by the work of Barber and Frye. Indeed, in my view, Barber and Frye can be seen together as a single influence, even though particular emphases in their criticism differ widely.

To this point in my argument, the position I take might be termed oppositional. I judge the emphasis on closure to be both inimical to the logic of criticism and contrary to the spirit and design of comedy. To some readers, my procedure may seem essentially negative. It is necessary, however, to clear away the critical ground in order to establish a different way of looking at the individual plays. It is precisely this work that the first chapter of the study accomplishes. Subsequent chapters focus on individual plays while keeping my main argument constantly in view. But that argument is seen in each case in the particular context of that comedy's critical history, and it leads directly into a discussion of the play that is intended to explore its particular strengths as comedy. I see this new focus as providing something like what Richard Levin calls for but does not himself provide in his discussion of the fundamental weaknesses of thematic criticism, a sense of the play in its moment-by-moment unfolding on the stage.

If the example of Levin provides one significant influence on my approach, the work of stage-centered critics like John Styan and John Russell Brown and (from a slightly different angle) Alexander Leggatt provides another. The five plays I discuss in detail are *The Merchant of Venice, Much Ado about Nothing, As You Like It, Twelfth Night,* and *Measure for Measure.* In every instance, I bring to my discussion of the play a sense of its critical history (including its stage history), and I work to demonstrate that as a comedy it creates its effects as it unfolds and not as it moves toward a significant and thematically crucial ending.

One effect of my reading is to restore to the comedies something of their joyousness, and in this too I find myself in opposition to one of the major trends of criticism of the last thirty years. That trend is, of course, the critical habit of finding in these works a darkness and a problematic quality that grows out of the need to make Shakespeare our contemporary. I don't wish to return to an age that one critic has referred to as the "lost innocence of criticism," a time "when we were advised to do little more than 'bask in the sunshine' of Shakespeare's comedies." But I do want to insist that the plays I discuss here are called comedies for a reason.

Thus I see the study as a whole performing a number of critical tasks. It offers a view of modern criticism of the comedies and describes how that criticism, dominated by the work of two men, has essentially led us away from the spirit of these plays toward a search for meaning and an assertion of their teleological design. It brings five representative comedies into a new perspective and illustrates how they unfold as works written for the stage. And, finally, in doing that critical work it restores to the comedies their true comic life.

Throughout this study, citations of Shakespeare's plays refer to the texts in *The Riverside Shakespeare*.

Shakespeare
AND
THE
ENDS
OF
Comedy

one

Crowning the End

The Aggrandizement of Closure in the Reading of Shakespeare's Comedies

ver thirty years ago, John Russell Brown reviewed the course of "The Interpretation of Shakespeare's Comedies: 1900–1953." In doing so, he located the central critical tendency of the works he surveyed in the "constantly repeated dictum . . . that the heart of Shakespeare's comedy lies in its characters."[1] This emphasis on character, he found, led to summary judgments about the plays' merits, including the view that "the endings of *The Two Gentlemen, Much Ado,* and *Twelfth Night* are . . . precipitous and unsatisfying." Faced with such evidence, his conclusion was a sort of wistful challenge: "There does seem to be something wrong with a theory of Shakespeare's comedy which implies that all his successes are so considerably blemished" (7).

Since that time, critical discussion of the comedies has been both abundant and varied. In 1979, Wayne A. Rebhorn reported that thirty-five books on the subject had appeared in the years after 1957, and the flood of interest has shown no sign of abating since that time.[2] But given all this activity, it remains curiously true that in the critical perspective afforded by most writers on Shakespearean comedy the plays are regarded as somehow falling short of the full glory that the form itself promises. In the most familiar readings, the comedies appear tainted by a sort of aesthetic original sin, a fault from which there is no redemption, since their shortcomings are measured against an ideal form that has declined to incarnate itself in the actual world of texts and theatrical representation.

If there is one root cause of this difficulty, it lies in the fact that the dominant approaches to comedy over the last three decades have attached extraordinary importance to the ways comedies end. Closure—and in this term I include the final disposition of characters, staging, tone, the completion of patterns of language and imagery, the characters' (or actors') relation to the audience, and any other matter that may be said to affect our final perception of a play's events—has become the focal issue in the criticism of Shakespeare's comedies. For some of the comic dramas this emphasis is of course not new at all. Dr. Johnson, one remembers, could not reconcile his heart to Bertram. But then he saw Shakespeare as generally content with unsatisfactory endings: "When he found himself near the end of his work, and in view of his reward, he shortened the labour, to snatch the profit. He therefore remits his efforts where he should most vigorously exert them, and his catastrophe is improbably produced or imperfectly represented."[3] The problem plays as a group, however large that group may be, have usually been faulted for not bringing their comic dilemmas to a satisfactorily comic issue; and Brown was simply acknowledging established practice when he treated them in a separate category in his review of critical interpretations.

But preoccupation with the endings of the romantic comedies has also been an insistent focus of criticism over the last three decades, with the result that nearly all the plays have been labeled as "problematic." Few readers today would willingly associate themselves with the emphatic cheeriness of J. Dover Wilson in his assertion that "the quality the first ten comedies have in common is happiness, a serene happiness, liable to develop into merriment in the conclusion."[4] It seems necessary, however, to divide the issues surrounding this emphasis on closure, to see that declaring the importance of the comedies' conclusions need not entail the view that the endings are dark or problematic or otherwise disturbing. To begin such a task, one need only look closely at the development of the critical situation in the years since Brown's survey. The focus on Shakespeare's characters has been replaced by other approaches, nearly all of them concerned in some way with dramatic structure; and at the source of these approaches stands the work of two key figures, C. L. Barber and Northrop Frye.[5] Although the particular emphasis of their analyses differs considerably—Frye focusing chiefly on literary antecedents, Barber taking a more "anthropological" way to his view of the comedies—both writers throw the weight of their observations on comic outcomes, the social reconciliation Frye discovers at the moment when "a new social unit is formed on the stage" ("Argument" 60) and the "clarification" Barber sees as the product of the characters' experience of "saturnalian release" (6–10).

For both Frye and Barber, then, closure stands for the comedies as "at once the source, and end, and test of Art."[6] Over the course of some years, Frye has refined and developed his interpretation of the comedies. In *A Natural Perspective* he offers not merely a fuller account of his understanding of the plays but an explanation of the critical logic that enables us to function as interpreters. In this view, our critical activity is in suspension during our experience of a literary work: we are in a "precritical" state, participating in a direct experience of the work's movement. Only when its structure becomes accessible to us can we engage in criticism proper. Thus Frye argues that "the point at which direct experience and criticism begin to come into alignment, in a work of fiction at least, is the point known as recognition or discovery, when some turn in the plot arrests the linear movement and enables us for the first time to see the story as a total shape, or what is usually called a theme" (9). One could hardly find a more definitive statement of the importance of closure. Barber's view, while similar, is in some ways more attentive to the complexity of a theatrical experience of the comedies; he pays more attention than does Frye to the mingling in Shakespeare of complementary views that are yet in some measure opposed, a quality of the plays defined recently with great skill by Norman Rabkin.[7] At nearly every stage of his discussion, Barber is careful to avoid overstatement. Thus he detects the problem one faces in concentrating on structure, he knows the sort of falsification it requires, yet he persists: "every new moment, every new line or touch, is a triumph of opportunism, something snatched in from life beyond expectation and made design beyond design. And yet the fact remains that it is as we see the design that we see design outdone and brought alive" (4). For both Barber and Frye, then, "the end crowns the work" is not merely an adage well suited to justify a critical procedure; it becomes instead the guiding principle of their criticism and enables them to find in the structure of Shakespearean comedies a teleological design.[8]

The influence of Barber and Frye on subsequent criticism is so widespread and profound as to make illustration nearly supererogatory. And even those critics whose aims are quite different from the aims of these two dominant figures tend to follow them in basing their assessments of the plays on the issue of closure. Thus Ralph Berry, who opposes himself directly to the "festive" readings of Barber and Frye, nevertheless makes closure the key element in his reading of the comedies: "I should prefer to see the conclusions of the middle comedies less as 'clarifications' than as provisional re-groupings of situations that will continue their complex development."[9] Similarly, Elliot Krieger, whose Marxist reading of the comedies emphasizes tensions and antagonisms undreamed of in the social worlds described by Barber and Frye, nevertheless finds the strongest confirmation of his thesis in Shakespeare's management of the plays' conclusions. Thus he says that the conclusion of *Twelfth Night* "confirms the aristocratic fantasy (Maria is, discreetly, kept off-stage) that clarification is achieved when people are released from indulgence and restored to the degree of greatness with which they were born."[10] Anthony B. Dawson may stand for all those critics who view comedy as a process whose end lies in some sort of discovery. For Dawson, "it is as if the characters must arrive, within the movement of the plot, at an understanding of, and response to, the nature of drama itself."[11] This emphasis on process, whether it leads to unmasking,[12] self-discovery, or some perception about the limitations of the theatre (as Philip Edwards would have it),[13] is clearly grounded in a teleological view of comedy: it is purposive, and its purpose is revealed in its close.

The comic dramatist described by W. Thomas MacCary is a very different figure from the Shakespeare of the critics I have just been discussing. MacCary's Shakespeare focuses not on marriage as a goal but on a passage through the stages of object-choice appropriate to a developing male; not on social integration but on narcissism.

And yet this playwright, too, focuses his comedies on a clear end: "the primary goal of the comedies, their teleology, is a definition of love, and this involves a consideration not only of stages in the development of object-relations but also some attention to pathology."[14] William C. Carroll, whose attention to metamorphoses in the comedies uncovers new insights on nearly every page, is likewise led to acknowledge that the changing shapes of love are finally brought to a static condition: "love is always harnessed, as Proteus was by Menelaus, into a single shape—into marriage, the final cause of comedy."[15]

The critics I have been discussing differ from Frye and Barber in a variety of ways. Some, such as Ralph Berry, deny the celebratory element in Shakespearean comedy in order to replace it with an emphasis on the problematic nature of the plays; yet such an approach still appeals to a reader's or spectator's perception of the individual comedy's end in an effort to establish its validity. Others, such as MacCary, wish to focus on something other than the social experience of the comedy, its communal meaning, and direct attention instead to the individual comic journey, the development of the central figure—in MacCary's case, the young male hero. But though MacCary takes note of stages in this progress, his chief concern is with the results at journey's end, the wholeness and personal integration of the hero.

It is even more clearly the case with those who accept the Barber-Frye position (if I may so label their views, conflated here for my immediate purpose) that the emphasis on closure so crucial to that position has been equally important to their refinements, extensions, and modifications of the outlines of "green world" and "festive" comedy. Among these writers I might include, following Rebhorn, critics of widely differing originality and importance: Blaze Bonazza, Charles R. Lyons, Patrick Swindon, and Leo Salingar.[16] Perhaps the most helpful illustration, though, appears in a recent book by Edward Berry in which he argues for "the romantic comedies as an unusually tight-knit genre based on specific ritual structures—those of initiation, courtship, and marriage."[17] Without wholly rejecting the insights of Barber and Frye, Berry insists on the primacy of personal rites over seasonal rites as the basis for our response to the comedies. His design, based on the studies of the anthropologist

Arnold Van Gennep, nevertheless shares the general outline made familiar by his predecessors, for he sees rites of passage and comic drama illustrating "a common evolutionary form—a form in which periodic forays into chaos lead to new kinds of integration" (8). Moreover, Berry emphasizes early in his book that he shares with Suzanne Langer a belief in the high significance of structure for an understanding of comedy, and he quotes approvingly her dictum: "Destiny in the guise of Fortune is the fabric of comedy" (7).

Because Berry presents his views with such elegance and subtlety, he affords the best starting point for illustration of what has often seemed a corollary to critical emphasis on closure in the comedies: the idea that Shakespearean comedy leaves us dissatisfied, unfulfilled, doubtful about the future of the comic protagonists and the world they inhabit, or simply aware—in a resigned, melancholy way—that the achievement of art is necessarily incomplete and insufficient for our needs in the world waiting outside the theatre. For Berry, though the "rite of incorporation" which is marriage provides an appropriate comic conclusion, "it is important to remember that the significance of a wedding lies in the full event, not merely in the abstract ideal it embodies. Since ideals are never actualized, weddings, like all ritual events, are inescapably ironic" (171). Later, he emphasizes the tonal complexity such endings provide: "We experience not only the delight that arises from comic communion but the detachment that accompanies our awareness of its incompleteness and fragility" (197). In support of this view he quotes an equally subtle critic, Philip Edwards, who claims that "the 'festive comedies' do not really end in clarification and in a resolution of the opposing forces of holiday and everyday. A strong magic is created: and it is questioned" (197, Edwards 70).

But if Berry and Edwards approach the issue of comic closure gingerly and analyze the presence of tonal richness with elegant tact, others are less subtle. The darkening of Shakespeare's comic endings has become a phenomenon not merely of critical discourse but, perhaps inevitably, of theatrical practice as well.[18] Perhaps no one has contributed to these linked tendencies with more energy and single-mindedness than Jan Kott. In the "Bitter Arcadia" he attributes to Shakespeare, Kott finds in every disguise a "diabolic invention" and "a call to orgy";[19] and nothing is more revealing of his emphasis on comedy's darkness than this summary of the mechanicals' play in *A Midsummer Night's Dream*: "The lovers are divided by a wall, cannot touch each other and only see each other through a crack. They will never be joined together. A hungry lion comes to the rendezvous place, and Thisbe flees in panic. Pyramus finds her blood-stained mantle and stabs himself. Thisbe returns, finds Pyramus's body and stabs herself with the same dagger. The world is cruel for true lovers" (190).

For Clifford Leech, this darkness is a progressive matter, shadowed only fleetingly in the early comedies but growing to such a point in *Twelfth Night* that "the most interesting thing" about the play "is its drawing back from a secure sense of harmony."[20] This reluctance to claim perfection—a reluctance that seems to be shared by the playwright and his comic dramas, functioning almost as autonomous creatures—manifests itself "alone among the early comedies" in *Love's Labour's Lost*, which "has a disturbing quality which we shall meet later: a recognition of unappeasable suffering, of death and recurrent destruction, of an imperfection that is not easily faced. As this strain grows in his comic writing, it makes Shakespeare's hold on the idea of comedy a precarious one" (25). Thomas F. Van Laan sees a similar evolution in Shakespeare's growth as a comic writer; thus "as Shakespeare's comedy reaches its full complexity, it also begins to take on some of the sombre colouring normally associated with the so-called dark comedies."[21] Less concerned with questions of the playwright's development, Richard A. Levin is forthright about his intention to develop only the antiromantic alternative of each of the plays (as though criticism were simply a matter of selecting alternatives). He does so by such dubious means as asserting that in *Much Ado about Nothing* "Shakespeare uses Margaret to develop the dark background against which Messina moves toward marriage."[22]

One final example may close this rather brief look at those critics who take an "antifestive" position on closure. Ralph Berry does so explicitly and with more than a touch of shrillness. He attacks with rhetorical questions: "What sort of double marriage is it that is thrown together at the end of *Twelfth Night*?" And lest some inattentive reader miss the point, he reiterates it with the aid of heavy sarcasm: "One can scarcely acclaim as the apotheosis of festivity a final dance from which the local lord of misrule is unavoidably absent, expiating in hospital his addiction to the pleasure principle" (13, 14). What Berry and others who share his view insist on is a Shakespeare far too knowing and worldly to support by his art the easy patterns of escape and fulfillment advocated by Frye and Barber and their followers. This Shakespeare is a doubter, a playwright who asks questions, a realist like Feste who knows all about change, about wind and rain, about mortality.

My object, though, is not to mediate these two commonly opposed ways of reading Shakespeare but to emphasize their common origin, to argue that it is precisely in its emphasis on closure that modern criticism of Shakespearean comedy has gone seriously off course, and to suggest by example a means of adjusting critical perceptions in order to correct this mistaken focus. Enough has been said, here and elsewhere, to show how completely the Barber-Frye position has become the orthodoxy of those who have written about Shakespearean comedy since that position was given its first statement. It is equally clear that those who have taken the opposite position have been forced to do so, for the most part, in a fashion that acknowledges their view as a heretical departure from an established system of belief. The cornerstone of that system, as I have tried to show, is the importance of structure, and especially of a design that issues in life-enhancing ceremony and clarification about the meaning of life itself. Thus both the followers of Frye and Barber and those who set themselves in opposition to their critical line have attributed to closure a signal importance.[23]

In the current critical situation, the description I provide cannot possibly cover every effort to come to terms with the comedies. What I am describing are the ways in which the dominant influences of Frye and Barber emerge in an emphasis on closure, and my focus therefore does not take into account critics who ignore altogether issues of design and structure. Nevertheless, the tendencies described here are both wide and deep. Even in cases where the critical method is little concerned with structural matters and therefore unlikely to stress closure, one still finds the influence of Frye and Barber. That influence is fully acknowledged by Peter Erickson, even though his larger concern with patriarchal structures would seem to ally him with forms of criticism that are less attentive to endings.[24] Marilyn Williamson, like Erickson focused on matters of patriarchy, has little apparent concern with structure. "The aim of [her book's] criticism," she writes, "is to demonstrate the contingency of the representation of power in the comedies and thereby to contribute to the feminist controversy about Shakespeare's representation of women and hierarchy."[25] Still, like most thematic critics, she does occasionally use language that locates meaning primarily in closure, making the comedies seem essentially teleological. Thus she describes what happens "as the comedies *drive toward* marriage" (36, italics mine); and she is even more explicit about the relationship of closure and meaning when she describes the end of *Measure for Measure*: "By reverting to the pattern of romantic comedy with the multiple marriages at the end, but with the marriages divorced from desire, Shakespeare makes even more striking the basic instability and tenuousness of the relationships, which exist by the ruler's order and trickery" (103).

Similarly, Adrian Louis Montrose is a critic whose attention to sociopolitical issues and whose general method associate him with the critical practices of the so-called new historicism; yet his reading of *As You Like It* depends heavily on detailed attention to closure and its thematic significance. In his formulation, comic form mirrors social process, enabling growth and change. Thus he argues that "the form of *As You Like It* becomes comic in the process of resolving the conflicts that are generated within it; events unfold and relationships are transformed in accordance with a precise comic teleology."[26] R. S. White, in *Shakespeare and the Romance Ending*, finds that Shakespeare, throughout his career, "worries away . . . at the problem of how to adopt into his dramatic endings the potential endlessness of romance."[27] This "constant worrying" is especially problematic for Shakespeare just because, in White's view, the comedies are, "in orthodox terms, defined in terms of their endings" (13). Thus the critical orthodoxy shaped by the work of Barber and Frye is seen retrospectively as a controlling aesthetic consideration for Shakespeare as he works to accommodate the pattern of romance with its "ancient endlessness" to "the dramatic necessity for a firm ending" (12–13).

What are the consequences of attaching such weight to closure? There are several, so varied that arranging them in a neat order presents some difficulty. Perhaps the most general consequence appears simply in the aggrandizement of the comic ending itself. By making the endings of his plays answer for so much, critics have imposed on Shakespeare an extraordinary burden. Bardolatry is not dead; it merely assumes, over the years, different forms. The bardolatry of these last decades, so far as Shakespeare the comic dramatist is concerned, grows out of the insistence that his comic endings be answerable both to his stature as our greatest playwright and to the full complexity of the plays as that complexity appears to the scrutiny of twentieth-century literary criticism and theory.

The simple fact is that Shakespeare, who has more to offer than most playwrights, is therefore asked to give us more than any playwright can legitimately be asked to give. He is in the position of the star pupil who so far outshines the others in the class that he is given not deserved praise but more difficult tasks. Pedagogically, and perhaps critically, such a procedure makes sense, but only to a certain point; after that it becomes not merely unfair but counterproductive. If we ask which comic writers could meet the standards imposed on Shakespearean closure, we could find, from the Renaissance to today, few names that any critic would advance with full confidence. Shakespeare's greatest rival in comedy, Ben Jonson, would surely not measure up. In *Every Man in His Humour*, Edward Knowell wins a bride who is a dramatic nullity, and Bobadill and Matthew are excluded from the final ceremony. In *Epicoene*, Dauphine dismisses Morose with the promise that he will not trouble him "till you trouble me with your funeral."[28] Jonson himself recognized that the close of *Volpone* might occasion criticism: "my catastrophe," he writes in the Epistle to that play, "may in the strict rigour of comic law meet with censure";[29] and Coleridge found that Jonson had erred in not making Celia Corvino's ward, so that she would be eligible for marriage to Bonario at the play's close. But Jonson, of course, wrote comedy of a different sort from Shakespeare's; his acerb, satiric comedy can hardly be faulted for not giving us festive endings.

What, then, of Lyly or Greene, Shakespeare's predecessors in romantic comedy; or what of Dekker, his contemporary? *Gallathea* comes to mind at once, for this play of sexual disguising, with its prominent threat of sacrificial death, its witty management of transvestism, and its touching allusions to absent siblings, contains many of the elements that Shakespeare capitalizes on in his plays. But Lyly's solution to the dramatic problems he creates for his characters is so patently artificial—one of the young women, we aren't told which, is to be metamorphosed into a young man—that we find in the comedy's close not an occasion for festivity but justification for assigning the play to a separate category, for thinking of it as masque or spectacle or show. Lyly fails to play the game by our rules; thus however delightful the close of *Gallathea* may be, it remains a feat of magic rather than a successful ending within the terms of the dramatic world that playwright has led us imaginatively to inhabit. It is as though Shakespeare, in *The Winter's Tale,* had allowed Paulina to reveal not a statuelike Hermione but an actual statue and had then allowed her to bring that statue to life.

Greene's *Friar Bacon and Friar Bungay* ends on a grand celebratory note. The play's final scene begins with a magnificent procession: "*Enter the* Emperor *with a pointless sword; next,* the King of Castile, *carrying a sword with a point;* Lacy, *carrying the globe;* Ed[ward]; Warr[en], *carrying a rod of gold with a dove on it;* Ermsby, *with a crown and scepter;* [Princess Eleanor], with the Fair Maid of Fressingfield *on her left hand;* Henry, Bacon, *with other Lords attending.*"[30] It continues with a chorus of mutual congratulation and self-congratulation among the members of the wedding party, then moves on through Bacon's prophecy to a closing note that unites wedding festivity with patriotic fervor:

> the time
> Craves that we taste of naught but jouissance.
> Thus glories England over all the west.
> (16.74–76)

Greene has written a wonderfully successful romantic comedy. But we should not forget that it includes the deaths of four minor figures (Lambert and Serlsby, *fils et pères*), the snatching off of Miles to hell, the arbitrary cruelty of Lacy to Margaret, and Margaret's disappointingly spiritless capitulation ("The flesh is frail") when faced with the choice between "God or Lord Lacy" (14.85, 83). Again, one sees in such a brief summary elements that will reappear in Shakespeare's comedies: the caddish male who nevertheless gains a bride he has willfully injured, a young woman whose acceptance of his hand is as sudden as it is unmotivated, and an atmosphere suffused with mistakings and deaths that would seem to question the very possibility of a comic end. Held to the requirements imposed on Shakespeare, Greene would be judged to have written a comedy whose festive end is insupportable—a failure on both moral and aesthetic grounds.

The Shoemaker's Holiday, Dekker's finest play, appeared in 1599, just at the point when Shakespeare was fashioning the greatest of his romantic comedies. A glance at the bare outline of the play reveals how similar it is to the mature achievements of Shakespeare in the genre. Like them, it involves a story of lovers separated by parental opposition and the demands of a harsh society; like them it mirrors the trials of those central lovers in the difficulties of another pair who are different in style and status; like them it includes a good deal of fooling by inventive and bawdy clown figures; and like them it involves a movement from one locale to a place of freedom and confusion, and then a movement back to the original locale, now transformed as it shapes itself to accommodate a changed set of values. But Dekker's play, for all its bumptious optimism, begins and ends with references to warfare. The second male lead, wounded in battle and changed beyond recognition, regains his wife through an elaborate stratagem designed by his fellow shoemakers and in the process dupes her suitor of both goods and money; and the ebullient Simon Eyre, with his egalitarian cry of "Prince am I none, yet bear a princely mind," gains his position as Lord Mayor and supports his princely style of entertaining with the help of inside information that might well be the envy of some of today's shadier Wall Street operators. Yet few critics would claim that Dekker's play is other than successful. On its own terms, and on the terms that we are likely to apply to its playwright, *The Shoemaker's Holiday* is a charmingly energetic comedy, peopled with characters who command our feelings of interest and affection and filled with incidents that seem nicely calculated to exploit and reward those feelings. Judged by the criteria ordinarily applied to Shakespearean comedy, however, the close of Dekker's play would come under more detailed scrutiny; and the play itself, victimized by a critical synecdoche that takes the part for the whole, would be judged to be flawed or problematic.

Thus one major consequence of a narrow focus on closure is the imposition on Shakespeare's comedies of an artificially high standard, one that no other comic writer is asked to reach. No doubt Shakespeare is a surpassing genius. As a comic dramatist, however, his is the same enterprise that other writers of comedy have engaged in over the years. Like Molière or Sheridan, Shaw or Alan Ayckbourn, Shakespeare in his comedies endeavors to fulfill the perennial aims of comedy. To fault him because in closing those endeavors of art he snatches his reward too hastily or artfully evades the moral or logical difficulties in his way is merely to bind Shakespeare in the chains of a bardolatry disguised as critical rigor.

The second consequence of the focus I have been describing exists on a different critical plane from the first. While the first concentrates attention on questions of achievement (How successful is Shakespeare as a comic dramatist?), the second directs scrutiny to questions of meaning (What is Shakespeare's final judgment about the issues he raises in this play?). This connection between closure and meaning is made strikingly clear in the words of Northrop Frye, quoted earlier, describing that point "when some turn in the plot arrests the linear movement and enables us for the first time to see the story as a total shape, or what is usually called a theme" (*Natural Perspective* 9). Almost any critic who follows Barber and Frye or who, in rejecting their views, bases a dissenting opinion on a differing interpretation of Shakespeare's handling of a particular comedy's end will be led to posit a similar connection between closure and meaning. The product of such a connection is not a matter of speculation; it is the assertion of "meanings" of the sort deplored by Richard Levin in his book *New Readings vs. Old Plays*.[31] For my purpose it is less important to record instances of such criticism than to show that, as they arise in discussions of Shakespearean comedy, they often (perhaps inevitably) grow out of a critical procedure that directs excessive attention to closure.

A remark by Joseph A. Bryant, Jr., focuses these issues very effectively. Writing of Shylock (but levying a requirement he clearly intends for the entire play), he says that "we can and should experience a series of widely differing reactions during the course of the play"; then he adds, "but if Shakespeare has done his work properly, the end should find them all focused in a single impression."[32]

This is teleological comedy in an emphatic form. The playwright's job is to mirror life in its complexity but, at the play's close, order it so that it may be read. Comedy is a puzzle to which closure provides the answer: "the end crowns the work."

Bryant's remark is especially useful just because critical responses to *The Merchant of Venice* offer striking documentation of what happens when closure is made to carry the whole burden of a comedy's meaning. A. D. Moody, in his short book on the play, declares an unwillingness to offer a simple, cynical view of *The Merchant of Venice*, one that would see it as being " 'about' " the way Christians succeed "by not practising their ideals of love and mercy" or "the essential likeness of Shylock and his judges."[33] Yet so exercised is he by those critics who, in his judgment, offer an opposed view that is equally simple in its romanticism or idealism that he seems driven to assert the cynical rebuttal in an aggressive fashion. Among the "romantic or idealizing" critics who are the villains of his piece, Moody numbers Sir Arthur Quiller-Couch, Frank Kermode, E. C. Pettet, C. L. Barber, and John Russell Brown, all of whom he cites for their falsification of the play's close. But Nevill Coghill, who finds in the play "the triumphant reconciliation of justice with mercy," earns the largest measure of Moody's scorn. Quoting Coghill's account of the comedy's final scene—"We return to Belmont to find Lorenzo and Jessica in each other's arms. Christian and Jew, New Law and Old, are visibly united in love. And their talk is of music, Shakespeare's recurrent symbol of harmony"[34]—Moody, equally persuaded that its meaning must be derived from its conclusion, challenges the romantic and idealizing critics on that ground. He does so by making Portia's fifth-act entrance a signal for the cessation of the music that Lorenzo calls for at 5.1.66–68. "With Portia's return," he argues, "we are brought back from thoughts of heavenly harmony to the sublunar world of mortals"; and further: "There is a harshness and dissonance in her devaluing the lark and the nightingale. . . . In the context just established this must make her 'fit for treasons, stratagems, and spoils'—which indeed is pretty much what she has been up to in Venice" (47).

Moody's detailed attention to Shakespeare's ending of *The Merchant of Venice* reinforces the trend in recent years of seeing all the comedies as incomplete or tinged with difficulty that may approach darkness. A. P. Riemer takes note of "a relatively recent orthodoxy . . . claiming that the final moments of Shakespeare's comedies represent an ironic, almost bitter commentary on one of the traditional ingredients of comedy: the insistence that all should end happily, that the characters, or at least the sympathetic ones, should be promised a life of perfect felicity" (10). Ralph Berry, viewing the same phenomenon from a different critical angle, remarks that "the leading theatrical practice of recent years . . . stresses the ironic and problematic aspects of the texts" (15). When that tendency merges with the practice of finding the plays' meanings crystallized in their closing moments, we have arrived at a critical situation answering to Frank Kermode's description: "The point is that all the comedies are 'problem' comedies; that *The Two Gentlemen of Verona* is a legend of Friendship . . . *A Midsummer Night's Dream* of love, *As You Like It* of courtesy, and *The Merchant of Venice* of justice"—where "legend" is assigned its Spenserian significance, and where the play's purpose in each instance is to move to a close that articulates its meaning.[35]

It happens that Anne Barton works out this stage of interpretation in an essay that employs Kermode's observations in another area altogether, the universe of prose fiction. Barton makes a primary distinction between the closure of tragedy and that of comedy. In tragedy, she claims, "In terms of individual consciousness, . . . fifth acts are true." Comedy presents a different case altogether: "Artistic forms which dismiss their characters into happiness . . . are far more problematic. Such endings . . . are a kind of arbitrary arrest. By means of art, the flux of life has been stilled."[36] The development Barton traces in Shakespearean comedy finds the plays up to *Twelfth Night* "essentially teleological"—i.e., they are "works of art in which a retrospective view from the final scene is encouraged, and alters our understanding of the play as a whole" (178, 179). But the withdrawal of Jaques at the end of *As You Like It* causes a "tremor in the balance of comedy" after which Shakespeare cannot sustain his earlier pattern. In *Twelfth Night*, then, we witness "a world of revelry, of comic festivity," fighting "a kind of desperate rearguard action against the cold light of day" (176). In this outline, Barton sees two sorts of endings: those before *Twelfth Night*, endings that, in Kermode's phrase, "frankly transfigure the events in which they were immanent" (*Sense* 175); and those found in *Twelfth Night* and the problem comedies that face us with a "divided fifth act" that "admits the fictional nature of the comic society" and forces the characters (some of them, at least) and spectators alike to confront the real world. It is clear, however, that both sorts of endings put strong pressure on closure: the first, Kermode's "immanent" ending, as it draws both events and their meanings to a point; and the second, Barton's, as it insists on meanings both within the play's world and in the world outside the theatre, "the world as it is" (179).

Intense scrutiny of comic closure has as its second consequence, then, the expectation that endings somehow encapsulate a play's meanings. Thus Gratiano's final pun in *The Merchant of Venice*, Malvolio's parting threat and Feste's song in *Twelfth Night*, Benedick's remarks to Don Pedro as the reformed bachelor initiates the marriage dance in *Much Ado about Nothing*, and the opposed songs that end *Love's Labor's Lost* all have been seen as the focal points of comprehensive—and contradictory—interpretations of those plays; and the list could be extended to include all the early comedies.

On one level, this desire to find encapsulated meaning at the plays' endings seems critically flawed when radically opposed meanings can be found emerging from the same textual materials. On another level, the didacticism of this approach almost always insists on the textual source of meaning and thus reduces the importance of the theatrical experience that ought properly to be seen as both the body and the soul of the comedy.

A third consequence of the habit of "crowning the end" appears in the mismatch between what might be called critical unitarianism (a desire to find in the comedies a tidy thematic focus, the "unified impression" of Bryant) and the sometimes unruly multiplicity of the plays themselves. As is usually the case, the problem comedies, especially *Measure for Measure*, illustrate this difficulty most strikingly. To accommodate the diversity of characters—with their weaknesses, obstinacies, unawarenesses, willful disobediences, and silences—to the Duke's self-assured remediation seems an overwhelming task on the stage. To gather such complexities within the boundaries of a single critical design seems even more difficult.

I discuss this notion more fully in the chapter devoted to this play. Here, it may suffice to say that as the comedies move in the direction of realism—as their worlds correspond more fully to societies in which men and women must work and live, and as those men and women seem to be judged appropriately by standards of psychological credibility—the reductionism of such teleological criticism seems less and less valid.

Measure for Measure, a critical hard case, is different only in degree from the earlier comedies in this respect. Yet precisely because of the play's multiplicity and felt complexity it urges the need for an alternative view of comedy. Such a view would not be teleological and focused on closure. Instead, it would allow consideration of the totality of Shakespeare's comedies, attending to them in their moment-by-moment release of comic energy and attending as well to the variety of characters and concerns they offer in such profusion. Readers of Alexander Leggatt's fine book on the comedies will see that I agree with him about the danger of seeking some "inner unity of the work of art." In such a search, "when everything is seen as contributing a central idea, a single pattern of images, or a particular kind of story, then individual scenes may be understood from that point of view alone, and thus denied their full life."[37] Freed from the unitary limitations of teleological criticism, one may find a wider and more generous, a more fully comic, perspective. In this perspective, it is possible to see that *Much Ado about Nothing* is, at some fundamental level of plot, "about" a variety of matters. These include the courtship of Claudio and Hero with its attendant mistakings and deceptions, the merry war of Beatrice and Benedick, Don John's villainy, the deception played out by Borachio and Margaret, Dogberry's maladroit efforts as watchman and reporter, Leonato's self-centered raging at his daughter's disgrace, and the fussy ineffectiveness of Antonio. *The Merchant of Venice* comes to a close in Portia's Belmont; but the city, with its inexplicable moods and its pervasive mercantilism, will not be denied. Shylock remains an almost palpable presence, and Antonio's ships are the subject of the title character's final speech. Lorenzo, having brought Jessica into the haven of a Christian community, nonetheless describes the comforts of Nerissa and Portia, "a special deed of gift, / . . . of all he [Shylock] dies possess'd of," as "manna" dropped "in the way / Of starved people" (5.1.292–95).

Given such richness, it is not at all surprising that unitarian critics are driven to extraordinary shifts as they try to fit the complex endings of Shakespeare's plays to their desire to see "the story as a total shape." A great many factors militate against this desire for order, beginning with Shakespeare's fondness for multiple plots. Thus *Twelfth Night*, sufficiently complicated in its chief romantic line with the interweaving of the affairs of Orsino and Olivia, Viola, and Sebastian, is made even more complicated by the very different courtship of Toby and Maria, the failures of Sir Andrew as wooer and duelist, and the duping of Malvolio. Viola is wise enough to realize that only time can untie her knotty difficulties; unitarian critics, less diffident, look to the play's closure to find a point where all of its complexities are resolved. The result in each case is intense critical pressure on a narrowly circumscribed set of data: the absence of Sir Toby and Sir Andrew (after 5.1.208), Maria's total absence in the final scene, Malvolio's exit line, the fate of the captain, Orsino's reluctance to allow Viola the hard-earned right to put "Cesario" behind her, and finally, Feste's song. One measure of the greatness of a play like *Twelfth Night* resides in its ability to endure and even to nourish such narrowly focused scrutiny. It seems worth pointing out that equally problematic and valuable critical issues present themselves in this play's early acts: Feste's absence from the letter scene; Olivia's easy forgetting of both her father and her brother; the curious fact that Orsino can seem, at one and the same time, to be a hopelessly inadequate suitor for Olivia and an ideal partner for Viola. On the other hand, the fact that honest and responsible critics can advance not merely opposed readings but a wide range of interpretations from the smallest details of the play's movement to an end seems to imply something about the fecundity of critical invention rather than about the inexhaustible richness of the text.

Shakespeare's plays are not merely texts, of course, as any number of stage-centered critics have demonstrated over the last twenty years or more—i.e., a period roughly coinciding with the critical emphasis on closure I have been describing here.[38] The widespread acceptance of the notion that we can understand plays more fully by attending to their theatrical elements than by concentrating on their verbal structure is often endorsed by critics who stress the importance of closure. Indeed, many of them employ such criticism as a key to interpretation of particular moments in a play's ending. But it seems difficult to ignore the irony involved in such a procedure; for while the two critical methods are not mutually exclusive, they are considerably at odds.

They are so because a play on stage (even if that stage is the critic's theatre of the mind) is a succession of dramatic moments involving the experience of all the theatrical resources that can affect its presentation. It is emphatically not a progress toward an end, especially in comedy. If the ending has a special importance, it remains firmly within the terms defined several years ago by Bernard Beckerman: "The finales of Shakespeare's Globe plays often fail to produce a climactic effect because the completion of the narrative does not arise from the conflicting forces of the theme or action. By the time the last scene began, the Elizabethan audience knew how the story would end. But it satisfied the Elizabethan sense of ritual to see the pageant of this conclusion acted out."[39] Critics who aggrandize closure, then, even if they acknowledge the need to consider the play's stage qualities, unnecessarily distort its shape and movement. What seizes our attention in the theatre is not a movement of plot or a progression of ideas but an actor's specific realization of a character's reason for being; the orchestrated perfection of a spying scene; moments of psychological and even physical sport released in a spirit of unrestrained exuberance. Examples are available in abundance: Launce and his dog in *The Two Gentlemen of Verona* (2.3.1–32); the academicians turned sonneteers in *Love's Labor's Lost* (4.3); the conclusion of the letter scene in *Twelfth Night* (2.5). For each of these illustrations Shakespeare furnishes many more in the same category, and the categories themselves only begin to suggest the sources of arresting theatrical pleasure everywhere available in the comedies. Such moments are scanted when critics throw the weight of their analysis on closure. Crowning the end, they undervalue the rich variety of event and character that gives to Shakespearean comedy its enduring appeal.

The consequences of emphasizing closure discussed up to this point are primarily matters that remain securely within the limits of critical discourse. One important result of that emphasis, however, breaks through those limits and leads to a fundamental confusion. Because a focusing on closure often implies formal resolution of a play's difficulties, it may lead to judgments about the settling of accounts, a sort of moral bookkeeping. How is Shylock left at the end of the play? Is Antonio's stipulation—that a more lenient punishment than the Duke's be pronounced if Shylock will convert—a gesture of mercy or a final cruelty imposed by the Jew's Christian tormentors? What are we to say of the marriages that close *Twelfth Night*? Can Maria have a reasonable hope that Sir Toby will reform, or Viola even imagine that Orsino will be mature and decisive enough to deserve her love, or Olivia put her faith in the still-dazzled Sebastian? Or, more important still, how can one acquiesce in Malvolio's banishment when even his mistress finds that he has been "most notoriously abused"? How can Hero accept Claudio, and how can we? What are we to make of Kate's abject capitulation, or Valentine's treating Sylvia as property when he offers to convey her to his treacherous friend Proteus, or the improbable repentance of Oliver?

Such questions are in some measure inescapable for anyone who takes the comedies seriously; but for critics who emphasize closure they are aggressively insistent, and they create special difficulties. In addressing issues of justice or raising supposititious questions about the future lives of comic characters, critics inevitably confuse the task of the playwright with other roles: moralist, counselor, psychologist. Only a short while ago, it seems, this point was so widely accepted as to seem self-evident. The work of art, self-contained and complete, did not and could not depend for its understanding on matters whose existence lay outside itself. The life of the characters in a fiction was understood to be coterminous with that fiction: one didn't ask if Claudio and Hero enjoyed their honeymoon or if Jessica eventually left Belmont, tired of the condescension of her Christian neighbors. But to observe all this is not to call for a return to an earlier and more comfortable critical faith; it is merely to say that a departure from such principles leads to confusion between the spheres of aesthetic design and moral judgment, between, in short, art and life.

And that is precisely the effect of much of the criticism that focuses on closure. What Shakespeare has joined together, critics willingly put asunder. Jessica is sure to awaken from her moonlit dream, and Portia is bound to recognize the mercantile basis of Bassanio's love. Kate will be herself again (if indeed her great speech is not a mere ruse), and Maria will grow tired of Sir Toby's drunken nonsense. A. P. Riemer has written effectively on this matter, and to persist at any length would be to cover ground that he has already traversed (5, 71, 110). It may be worth pointing out, however, that in this joining of the issues of closure and judgment all the comedies are likely to seem, as Frank Kermode has found them to be, essentially problematic. Taken to its critical extreme, an interest in closure may even lead one to believe, with Zvi Jagendorf, that "a study of comic endings is really a study of the mode itself."[40] Understanding the consequences of aggrandizing closure should not lead one to deny the importance of the way Shakespeare's comedies end. Revenge, in Kyd's *Spanish Tragedy*, pronounces "a version of one of the commonest sayings" when he mollifies the impatient ghost of Andrea with the assurance that "the end is crown of every work well done."[41] But to elevate closure further, to crown the end rather than to see it as a necessary and inevitable part of the total work, is to pervert a commonplace and to distort both the nature and the function of Shakespeare's comedies. These comedies are not driven toward their endings; they are, rather, driven by their ends. It is no mere pun to say that these are very different matters. In the chapters that follow, my chief effort will be to amplify the difference between them.

two

"A wild of nothing, save of joy"

The Comic Pleasures of The Merchant of Venice

hakespeare the comic playwright and Shakespeare the tragic dramatist have long been judged differently. Everyone remembers Dr. Johnson's observation that "in tragedy he often writes with great appearance of toil and study, what is written at last with little felicity; but in his comick scenes, he seems to produce without labour, what no labour can improve." Equally memorable is Johnson's further judgment that "his tragedy seems to be skill, his comedy to be instinct."[1] In twentieth-century criticism of Shakespeare, one finds a similarly clear distinction between the evaluations of the comedies and the tragedies. This is not, however, a matter of preferring Shakespeare's achievement in one dramatic kind over his work in the other. Rather, it is that the critical approaches to tragedy are enormously varied, while discussions of the comedies are dominated by two seminal figures whose work shares a single and directive emphasis. No general treatment of the tragedies has succeeded in gaining the endorsement of a wide public from among the readers of Shakespeare or the canonization conferred by the adoption of its method among those writers and scholars who support and extend the critical tradition. A. C. Bradley's *Shakespearean Tragedy* is no doubt for both groups an inescapable influence, but that great book represents the end of a line in criticism, its last brilliant expression, and not a beginning. After Bradley, though one may point to substantial achievements, there is nothing like a dominant view or a compelling method.

In comedy, the case is quite different. Before the Second World War, criticism of the comedies was neither extensive nor deep. Beginning in the late 1940s—coincident, that is, with the expansion of the university system in the United States and the widespread professionalization of literary studies in all the major English-speaking countries—Shakespeare's comedies came under increasing scrutiny. But although this growing attention, noticed first by John Russell Brown in 1955, has continued uninterrupted to the present day, its development has been shaped, and in large measure controlled, by the critical approaches of two men, Northrop Frye and C. L. Barber.[2] Chapter 1 provides a survey of the widespread influence of Barber and Frye, documenting the ways in which their views have directed subsequent critics of the comedies to concentrate on the relation of meaning and closure. It seems unnecessary to repeat that argument in full detail, but it does seem useful to stress once again a significant anomaly arising from the aggrandizement of closure: the fact, to put it bluntly, that such an emphasis supports equally well those who find the comedies festive and those who find them dark and problematic. Before turning to *The Merchant of Venice,* it may be useful to point out some instances in which opposed readings of individual plays find their major support in a play's ending and even, within that ending, in identical details.

A Midsummer Night's Dream provides a striking example. Barber describes how, in "the final dancing blessing of the fairies," they "have been made into tutelary spirits of fertility, so that they promise" the lovers that "the blots of Nature's hand / Shall not in their issue stand." He goes on to describe the kinds of dances the fairies' language would likely lead to as Shakespeare shifts, in the play's close, "from a fully dramatic medium to conclude, in a manner appropriate to festival, with dances and song" (138). Almost anything Jan Kott says about the play could be set over against this view, but Kott provides too easy a contrast and, for many readers, is perhaps too shrill and obsessive to function as a helpful example. Instead, here is a comment from a less aggressively single-minded critic, attending to essentially the same moment remarked by Barber: "Even at the end, when they [the fairies] come to bless the wedding, they remind the audience of their potential malevolence."[3] In a recent bibliography of work on *A Midsummer Night's Dream* since 1940, one of the editors endorses the practice that leads to such observations, to the locating of a play's "meaning" at the point of closure. "The fairies," writes D. Allen Carroll, "by streaming on stage to bless the marriage bed after Theseus' departure, appear to represent Shakespeare's last word on what constitutes reality, at least *within* the play."[4]

Twelfth Night affords a variety of similar examples. Critics may focus, at the close, on Malvolio and his place in the play's world; on the lovers, and the suitability of the marital arrangements (including the union of Sir Toby and Maria); and on Feste's final song. The following comments suggest, in brief compass, the variety of conclusions such emphases may produce:

> Malvolio . . . comes as a figure of violence and leaves unreconciled, meditating a futile revenge. For him too, the dream is over and the moment of awakening bitter. Jaques had walked with dignity out of the new society; Malvolio in effect is flung.[5]

> We have seen in the play as a whole the power of conventional images to touch their hearers. The same may be true of the stylized image of the lovers in the final scene: the fact that it is obviously a matter of literary artifice does not make it invalid; on the contrary, its bold stylization strikes through to the heart of experience.[6]

> Nor should the autumnal mood of Feste's final song disturb our pleasure in the play. . . . If he knows that no festivity can put a stop to time, this is not to detract from time's benign moments, but to make them doubly valuable.[7]

> Malvolio in the end is neither crushed nor pacified. He belongs . . . to the world of law and business, outside the circle of the play.[8]

Whatever the specific meaning such comments suggest, they are alike in sharing the view that the comedy's significance is chiefly discoverable in the details of its closure.

In recent years, an extraordinary amount of critical pressure has been directed to the close of *The Merchant of Venice*. Norman Rabkin has written brilliantly of this play's richness, seeing its complexity as reflecting and even equivalent to the complexity of life itself.[9] Most critics, however, are less content than Rabkin to see comedy as a means of exploring questions and regard the form instead as involved in supplying answers. Thus Joseph A. Bryant, Jr., writing of Shylock but clearly thinking of the play as a whole, acknowledges the work's richness: "If we read or see [it] without the impediment of artificially imposed restraints, we can and should experience a series of widely differing reactions during the course of the play." "But," he goes on to say, "if Shakespeare has done his work properly, the end should find them all focused in a single impression. Otherwise, we have a choice of Shylocks and a choice of plays, and any *Merchant of Venice* that satisfies us must be a reduction."[10]

Bryant's analysis, put forward as a solution to a problem in critical method, serves instead to reveal a more fundamental problem. If the key to a play's meaning lies in a final, single impression, its end is likely to be subjected to extraordinarily intense critical scrutiny. Furthermore, since such attention is shaped and conditioned by whatever method a particular critic has chosen in pursuing the study of the comedy up to that point, the outcome seems necessarily a matter of multiple, even contradictory, interpretations. This can be illustrated by a quick second look at two critics who have made *The Merchant of Venice* a subject of detailed critical attention. Although I discuss their opposing views in chapter 1, I want to bring them into the argument at this point precisely because they offer a paradigmatic instance of the critical situation I am describing here.

The first of these writers is A. D. Moody, who in his short book on the play feels called upon to assert what he calls the "cynical" view of the work over against the "romantic and idealizing" critics and scholars who, he believes, have distorted its meaning.[11] The second is Lawrence Danson, who wisely declines to wrangle with Moody, but who nevertheless takes a quite different view from his, finding in the comedy's close "Touches of Sweet Harmony."[12] The two critics could hardly be more unlike in their approaches to the play, in their prose styles, and in the tones they communicate throughout their books. Moody adopts the role of the defender of truth, besieged on every side by critical ninnies and knaves. He has a view—and critical values—to uphold, and he will do so even in the face of strong opposition and a blind refusal of others to see the truth. Danson, by contrast, is civility itself. He finds *The Merchant of Venice* a source of delight, and he writes to communicate that delight to others, hoping they will then be able to share it with him. Yet they are alike in this: each of them looks to the play's close for evidence designed to clinch his interpretation. Moody finds that an emphasis on irony is one way to "get close to the final effect of the play," and he quotes approvingly John B. Shackford's judgment: "Inside the hollow heart of the conventional action the harmonious notes of Christian love echo with ironic discord" (52–53).[13] Danson, on the other hand, finds fulfillment and harmony just at those points where Moody locates ironic tension. For Danson, "In its smallest details of action and language the play's final scene simultaneously sounds a satisfyingly resolving chord and carries its musical suggestiveness beyond the reach of discursive language" (194).

These descriptions seem to be setting before us two very different plays. Such a result is nearly inevitable when closure, seen as the locus of meaning, is asked to answer for so much. This insistence on revelations of meaning at the play's close converts comic endings into instruments of teleological design and transforms elements of dramatic structure into vehicles of thematic purpose. What gets lost when closure receives such emphasis is the very heart of comedy, its moment-by-moment development on the stage as it provides its assortment of theatrical pleasures. These pleasures are not always of the same kind: a play such as *A Midsummer Night's Dream* offers a range of spectacle and subtleties of tone unattempted in *The Taming of the Shrew*, in which Shakespeare works masterfully with the elements of physical farce. The relatively realistic *Much Ado about Nothing* affords brilliant wit combats between Beatrice and Benedick, while *As You Like It*, in Rosalind, illustrates something like a female fantasy of how such combats should be conducted, judged, and rewarded.

What, then, are the comic pleasures of *The Merchant of Venice*? And how can our attending to such pleasures take the burden off closure and help us to see the play not as a purposive design moving toward an end in which its significance will be revealed but as the "actual dramatic experience in its concrete particularity" that Richard Levin has suggested should be the source of our interpretations of the plays of Shakespeare and his fellow dramatists?[14] These two questions derive from two related but wholly different orders, and a response to the first is required preparation for any suggestions about the second. It seems necessary, therefore, to explore the comic workings of the play, to identify the major sources of its particular effects, and to relate these effects to its overall theatrical design.

Bertrand Evans, over thirty years ago, put forward an analysis of Shakespeare's comic practice that still seems fundamentally correct. In his view, the central feature of the playwright's technique in comedy is the employment of "discrepant awareness," the use of disparities in knowledge among the various audiences, onstage and off, about the succession of transactions that make up the comic plot.[15] Although Evans's own analysis leads him to find that in *The Merchant of Venice* Shakespeare "relies less on exploitation of discrepancies than in any other comedy after *Love's Labour's Lost*" (46), the function of onstage audiences is nevertheless crucial to the play's comic success.

Almost no one—and none of the main plot figures—occupies the stage alone in *The Merchant of Venice*. The two exceptions are Launcelot Gobbo, for the first thirty lines of 2.2, and Jessica, at the close of 2.3 (lines 15–21) and again at 2.5.56–57. Launcelot's solo performance is a comic turn that almost seems, in the play's total economy, sheer lagniappe. Launcelot's final decision in the little moral drama he reprises for the theatre audience—to disregard conscience, hearken to the fiend, and abandon Shylock—may supplement other negative judgments about the money-lender, but in light of the play's other events, the servant's judgment is hardly crucial in shaping an audience's view of his master. Jessica's two brief moments alone on the stage serve primarily to control our perception of 2.5. At the end of 2.3, having sent Launcelot off with a message for Lorenzo, she announces her intention to leave Shylock and marry Lorenzo. In a quite different tone from Launcelot's reported disputation between the fiend and his conscience, her resolve nevertheless reflects a similar tension, here between the demands of blood and those of behavior:

> Farewell, good Launcelot.
> Alack, what heinous sin is it in me
> To be ashamed to be my father's child!
> But though I am a daughter to his blood,
> I am not to his manners. O Lorenzo,

> If thou keep promise, I shall end this strife,
> Become a Christian and thy loving wife.
>
> (15–21)

This announcement, as Evans demonstrates, conditions our perception of 2.5, where Shylock—ridiculing Launcelot's decision to leave, worrying over the invitation to sup with Antonio and Bassanio, and fussing about the security of his house and goods—is wholly ignorant of the impending loss of his daughter. The rote wisdom that marks his exit—

> Fast find, fast bind—
> A proverb never stale in thrifty mind.

—Jessica caps with a couplet of her own:

> Farewell, and if my fortune be not cross'd,
> I have a father, you a daughter, lost.
>
> (54–7)

that marks this scene with its final economic irony.

"Discrepant awareness" of this kind, though, where we as an audience judge a character's behavior in light of superior knowledge we share with another character or characters, is not a major feature of *The Merchant of Venice*. Yet the use of audience is crucial to the play's comedy. Almost every major action in the play, and many of its subsidiary events, take on a particular coloring from the presence of an audience. The most private feelings—of distress, insecurity, love, elation—take place in view of others, become nearly public. Antonio's melancholy, inexplicable but profound, is subject to discussion equally by acquaintances and old friends. Given its emphasis at the beginning of the play, it seems a prominent topic of conjecture on the Rialto, almost as significant a matter of gossip in Venice as the state of his mercantile affairs. Salerio and Solanio devote their time on stage in the first scene to canvassing possible reasons for Antonio's sadness, which they find as wearying as he does. Then, at the approach of Bassanio, Lorenzo, and Gratiano, they take their leave, each of them deferring to the new arrivals. Solanio describes the newcomers as "better company"; Salerio declares:

> I could have stay'd till I had made you merry,
> If worthier friends had not prevented me.
> (1.1.60–61)

In the scene's next stage, Lorenzo speaks only to attend to necessary business and excuse his silence, while Gratiano, whose loquaciousness is the subject of some humor, expatiates at length on Antonio's mood and advises him to "fish not with this melancholy bait / For this fool gudgeon, this opinion" (101–102). The third and final stage of the scene leaves Antonio and Bassanio together. After Bassanio apologizes for Gratiano's babbling, Antonio opens the topic that seems to many critics the source of his unhappiness:

> Well, tell me now what lady is the same
> To whom you swore a secret pilgrimage,
> That you to-day promis'd to tell me of?
> (119–21)

Bassanio responds to this behest somewhat indirectly, taking nearly forty lines to describe his financial shortcomings and prepare his friend for yet another request for monetary assistance before he gets to the beginning of his promised report: "In Belmont is a lady richly left" (161).

A review of the events of this first scene suggests that Antonio's sadness is both explained and, to a great extent, dissipated by Shakespeare's use on stage of a performer-audience relationship. Salerio and Solanio have apparently been engaged before their entrance in an effort to prise out the reasons for Antonio's melancholy, and he agrees that their impatience with his behavior is understandable: "It wearies me, you say it wearies you" (2). They continue their efforts in dialogue that suits their frequent casting in productions as a comic team. In effect, they put on a show for Antonio, reinforcing one another's observations and supplying an energy that refuses to allow his lassitude its dampening dominance. After Solanio and Salerio exit, Gratiano continues their function, even extending their catalogue of "strange fellows" whose behavior is inexplicable or perverse. Again, Gratiano is performing here, addressing his remarks chiefly to Antonio while looking to Bassanio and Lorenzo for approval of his efforts. The effect of this dramatic tactic is twofold: a gradual narrowing of focus as Antonio moves in stages from a nearly public to an intensely private relationship (from Salerio and Solanio to Bassanio), and a distancing of the issue of "sadness" that keeps it at a level of particularity and comic comment and prevents it from establishing itself as the key element of the play's atmosphere. When at last Antonio and Bassanio are alone, the merchant's first words are

> Well, tell me now what lady is the same
> To whom you swore a secret pilgrimage.
> (119–20)

That introductory "Well" speaks volumes. It expresses relief: now that the two friends are alone, the issue troubling Antonio can be brought into the open. It suggests obligation: as a friend, Bassanio owes Antonio an explanation of his decision to attempt such a pilgrimage. And it suggests impatience: we both know all about Gratiano, Antonio seems to say; now let's turn to the main business—i.e., to what is bothering me. Surprisingly, once Bassanio does so (after a good deal of "circumstance" that may simply reflect his embarrassment at asking for financial help), Antonio's sadness disappears as both issue and behavior. Spurred to action by his friend's needs, he exits on an upbeat note, focused on the task at hand:

> Go presently inquire, and so will I,
> Where money is, and I no question make
> To have it of my trust, or for my sake.
> (183–85)

The use of an audience-spectator relationship on stage, especially in the scene's last phase, with Bassanio as storyteller in a command performance for Antonio, suggests how skillfully Shakespeare uses this theatrical device as a means of controlling tone. By the scene's close, the false dramatic problem of Antonio's sadness has been dispensed with, and in its place we have a far more difficult problem—how to acquire the necessary backing for Bassanio's quest—whose answer will unfold complexities resolved only in the trial scene.

By labeling Antonio's sadness "a false dramatic problem" I do not, of course, mean to suggest that it is without interest as a critical issue and as a theatrical question that requires resolution. The possible homoerotic attraction between the two men (or of one to the other) has been a significant part of the play's stage history. Whatever the nature of the bond between them, Antonio's "Well, tell me" may be seen as a recognition of the superior power of Bassanio's attraction to Portia and the scene's energetic and lightened close as testimony to the persuasive function of Bassanio's onstage performance.

Any number of critics have claimed that 1.2 begins on the same note as the previous scene, with Portia's "my little body is a-weary of this great world" providing not merely a verbal echo of Antonio's entrance lines but a tonal reminiscence as well. The corollary, for most such commentators, is that "sadness" rules in both Venice and Belmont. But Portia's mood, like Antonio's, shifts as she is subjected to the witty maneuvering of Nerissa. The balanced dialogue of lady and waiting-woman (1–34) gives way to Portia's descriptions of her suitors, each prefaced by a question from Nerissa. The effect on the audience is that of watching a sort of witty catechism, well-rehearsed and familiar but still pleasurable to questioner and respondent, while the effect on the participants is to move them, through shared fun, to a point at which Bassanio, "the best deserving a fair lady," is called to mind. Thus the play's second scene does reflect the first, but not in a fashion that sustains an atmosphere of sadness or a wearying melancholy. Rather, the scene exhibits the energy and animation love can infuse into youthful spirits; and it ends, as does its predecessor, on a note of purpose and bright movement. It takes no great depth of reading skill or familiarity with comic conventions to recognize that Portia's ready admission—"I remember him well, and I remember him worthy of thy praise" (120–21)—is a sure guarantee not only that Bassanio will have "the means / To hold a rival place" with the "renowned suitors" for her hand but that his quest will be successful. This, it seems to me, is the function of the parallelism in the scenes, of their similarities of device and structure.

The key device, or dramatic tactic, is Shakespeare's use of an onstage audience. He continues to employ it throughout the play, notably in the casket scenes, in the courtroom scene, and in the conclusion, where Bassanio and Gratiano, having given away the pledges of their love, must confess to Portia and Nerissa that they have parted with their rings. At each of the play's crucial moments, in other words, Shakespeare designs matters in such a way that he distances his audience from the action, enabling us as readers or viewers to judge the events from a remove, seeing on one side of the exchange a performer or performers (whose skills we, along with the characters in the onstage audience, may judge) and on the other side an audience (who may or may not share with us foreknowledge of the performer's limitations or the sources of that character's script). When we do have such awareness, as in the closing scenes, the effect is to validate our comic trust, to confirm our faith that, as Bertrand Evans would have it, "the world of *The Merchant of Venice* is one in which goodness and mirth prevail" (66).

This device of the onstage audience is the key to understanding the scenes with Morocco and Arragon; and although those scenes ask for different treatments in the theatre, they may be discussed together to good critical purpose. Morocco's attempt to choose the right casket (2.7) is well prepared for. Shakespeare mentions him first in 1.2, when Portia responds to news of his impending arrival with a racial remark: "if he have the condition of a saint, and the complexion of a devil, I had rather he should shrive me than wive me" (129–31).

A short scene, 2.1 is given over to formal exchanges between Morocco (who enters with his followers) and Portia (with Nerissa and other attendants). It allows Shakespeare to spell out the conditions that the suitors must accept, but more significantly it allows him to illustrate Portia's scrupulous attention to the requirements of her father's will. She is gracious and polite to Morocco, assuring him that the man who wins her, whatever his color, "then stood as fair / As any comer I have look'd on yet / For my affection" (2.1.20–22). Yet at Morocco's subsequent appearance (2.7) and at the trial of Arragon (2.9), neither the harshness of the will's conditions nor Portia's willingness to stick to her share of the bargain has the dominant effect on our perception. Instead, the primary shaping forces of our view are Portia's earlier satiric descriptions of the retiring suitors and the mingled attitudes of Portia and Nerissa, compounded of mockery and trepidation, as they watch each suitor approach the caskets and attend to the logic that will direct his choice.

Certainly the influences I have just described control most stage versions of these scenes. The Morocco in Olivier's National Theatre production was only an extreme manifestation of the ethnocentrism and racial stereotyping that customarily define that character's role.[16] Arragon, often a mustachioed dandy, may be asked to lisp his way through the thicket of *s*'s in the schedule he finds in the silver casket. But it is not merely theatrical tradition that leads us to see the scenes in this way; a more fundamental cause is Shakespeare's use of an onstage audience. In this case, that tactic is joined to Shakespeare's use of comic preparation in a way that both shapes and determines the scenes' tones and directs our judgment.

Preparation for the comic dimension of the two casket scenes begins in 1.2 with Portia's catalogue of unwelcome suitors. The Neapolitan Prince, the County Palentine, the French lord, Monsieur le Bon, Falconbridge, the Scottish lord, and the Duke of Saxony's nephew make up a gallery of stereotyped portraits. While the Neapolitan Prince is obsessed with his horse, a creature which is his sole source of converse and value, the French suitor is devoid of fixed ideas and so given to mimicry that he has no character at all. The young baron of England borrows his clothing from all the countries he visits but seems incapable of gathering even a scrap of their languages. Each figure has the faults of his country, and Portia ends her comic analysis with the drunken German, telling Nerissa in mock horror, "I will do any thing, Nerissa, ere I will be married to a spunge" (98–99).

Thus when the unwelcome suitors, Morocco and Arragon, come to take their chances in choosing a casket, Shakespeare has already provided a context in which to judge them. In 2.7, Portia says little; she seems content to direct Morocco to his task, open the golden casket once he makes his choice, and express her relief at his departure. The bulk of the scene is taken up with Morocco's speeches: his lengthy process of decision making and his reading and response to the scroll. But the scene enacts a contest, even a kind of ritual, witnessed by the trains of Portia and the prince. As observers of that contest, Portia and Nerissa watch the performance put on by Morocco.

Shakespeare gives few verbal clues to their behavior, yet it seems clear that the combination of earnest concern and mockery seen in 1.2 operates in this instance as well. Portia's derisive account of her earlier suitors prepares for her attitude toward Morocco here, and though that mockery is not articulated verbally, it has full opportunity for nonverbal expression during the ponderous and heavily rhetorical self-questioning of the prince. John Styan suggests that "the ceremonial of the three fairy-tale casket-scenes in *The Merchant of Venice* . . . may have matched the rhetoric of the foreign princes' speeches with suitably exotic splendour."[17] This is undoubtedly the case, but that splendor is itself necessarily viewed in the context of the xenophobic jesting of 1.2 and the by-play allowed to Portia and Nerissa as Morocco enacts his laborious decision making.

While Morocco's scene is well prepared for both by the comments of 1.2, which provide a context of mockery, and by his arrival in 2.1, Arragon's casket scene (2.9) is a hastier affair. Yet it takes advantage of the same dramatic preparation that governs our view of Morocco's performance. If the earlier suitor offers a target for ridicule in his self-important oratory, a comic Othello expending rhetorical riches in a little room, Arragon provides an even more inviting mark in his boasting self-righteousness. Distracted easily by the appeal of simile ("like the martlet," 28 ff.), he loses his way like some doddering figure from Chekhov when a didactic point claims his attention:

> Let none presume
> To wear an undeserved dignity.
> O that estates, degrees, and offices
> Were not deriv'd corruptly, and that clear honor
> Were purchas'd by the merit of the wearer!
> How many then should cover that stand bare?
> How many be commanded that command?
> How much low peasantry would then be gleaned
> From the true seed of honor? and how much honor
> Pick'd from the chaff and ruin of the times
> To be new varnish'd? Well, but to my choice.
> (39–49)

And Portia, her mocking judgment confirmed, pronounces finally on both unsuccessful suitors:

> O, these deliberate fools, when they do choose,
> They have the wisdom by their wit to lose.
> (80–81)

Bassanio's casket scene (3.2) is another matter altogether. One of Shakespeare's great gifts as a comic playwright is his sure control of tone. Here that gift is revealed in the strikingly different atmosphere of a scene that we have already witnessed twice. Mockery is behind us. Gratiano and Nerissa, great talkers both, keep silence. Portia, having declared her love, but having declared too her commitment to the terms of her father's will, sends Bassanio to the contest:

> Live thou, I live; with much, much more dismay
> I view the fight than thou that mak'st the fray.
> (61–62)

Suspense joined to mockery defined the tone of the earlier casket scenes. Now the tone is suspense and a sort of constrained joyousness that struggles for release. Portia is emotionally *with* Bassanio in his deliberations; and Nerissa, formerly her partner in mockery, is now one with Gratiano, silently hoping for a choice that will ratify their own election. The performance of Bassanio, enriched by the music Portia calls for at line 43, is a meditation on that most familiar of Shakespearean themes, seeming and substance. Dismissing "ornament" from the beginning, Bassanio moves inexorably to choose the leaden casket and, by his choice, to release in Portia the joy that is the consequence of his right determination:

> O love, be moderate, allay thy ecstasy,
> In measure rain thy joy, scant this excess!
> I feel too much thy blessing; make it less,
> For fear I surfeit.
> (111–14)

The comedy of this third casket scene, then, once again works through the device of an onstage audience. But while the earlier uses of this device work primarily to create a distance—to make us see the performer *through* the onstage audience—in this case our attention is focused primarily on the spectator, here Portia, whose reactions determine the scene's tone. A similar use of this tactic appears in *Twelfth Night* 2.4, a scene also controlled in part by music, where our judgment of Orsino is reshaped as we register chiefly not his performance but Viola's response to it.

This tactic of presenting characters as performers whose action is judged by an onstage audience achieves a different sort of intensity in act 4. Before the trial scene, in 3.1 and again in 3.3, Shakespeare reveals the implacability of Shylock, whose loss of Jessica reinforces his hatred of Antonio and whose loss of ducats makes the destruction of his rival a more compelling need; "for were he out of Venice," says the Jew, "I can make what merchandise I will" (3.1.27–29).

This preparation—"comic preparation" seems less than exact, though the events issue in comedy—continues in 4.1 before Shylock's entrance with the Duke's description of him as

> A stony adversary, an inhuman wretch,
> Uncapable of pity, void and empty
> From any dram of mercy.

and Antonio's resolution:

> I do oppose
> My patience to his fury, and am arm'd
> To suffer, with a quietness of spirit,
> The very tyranny and rage of his.
> (4–6, 10–13)

The Duke's address to Shylock momentarily suspends our expectation; knowing full well the rigidity of Shylock's attitude, the Duke pretends that "the world thinks" Shylock's aim is mercy and that "we all expect a gentle answer" (17, 34). This gambit, though, seems only to increase Shylock's pleasure in his own performance. His taunting assertion of absolute power (if it is not a defense of whimsy)—"say it is my humor"—deliberately avoids the Duke's request, though "now for your answer" and "are you answered?" suggest an effort to respond. Bassanio correctly judges that "this is no answer"; but Shylock, certain of his legal position, dismissively responds, "I am not bound to please thee with my answers!" (43, 52, 62, 63, 65).

Like Morocco and Arragon earlier in the play, Shylock is given performance space in which to reveal his values. In their speeches, the suitors displayed their logical powers and paraded their self-regard; Shylock flaunts his personal superiority and the strength of his case before the court. Inevitably, we see his performance in the light of theirs and anticipate that he will suffer a similar deflation. The arrival of Nerissa affirms the rightness of this expectation, and it seems appropriate that her entrance just precedes Gratiano's first words in the scene. His outburst, generated by the anger that will later, at Shylock's overthrow by the law, be transformed into cruel mockery, also signals a shift in the scene's control. Shylock continues to be the chief performer in the scene, but he is joined by Portia, who functions as both playwright and onstage director. Bertrand Evans describes this scene well, tracing the offers Portia makes to permit Shylock "to prove his affinity with humankind" (64). Our pleasure in Portia's manipulative skills is the comic counterpart to the horror we feel as Iago stages his playlet with Cassio in 4.1, inviting Othello as spectator to enact in physical terms a transformation to animality that will soon reveal itself in his language and behavior: "Do but encave yourself" (81).

Enough has been written about the trial scene over the years to make it clear that no single account of its effects can be persuasive. Lawrence Danson points to our shifting view of Shylock, and the way he gains our sympathy as he loses power, especially since Gratiano underscores that loss of power with such savage taunting. Norman Rabkin has written with compelling clarity of the scene, arguing that Shakespeare refuses to allow his spectators an unequivocal attitude toward the Jew. What is there in the trial scene that keeps it in the realm of comedy? More than anything else, I think, it is Shakespeare's placing of Shylock in a performing stance, a tactic that distances him from us and forces us to see him through the eyes of the characters who share the stage with him.

In the early part of the scene, comic preparation and his similarity to the failed suitors condition our view; in the latter part, our attention is focused through Portia, who conducts the trial with majestic assurance and equanimity but at the same time uses her authority to control the scene's pace and therefore its comedy. Nearly everything she does, in speech or action, carries the potential for comic effect, beginning with her disingenuous question, "Which is the merchant here? and which the Jew?" (174). Her strict legalism, prompting Shylock to burst out in praise of this "Daniel come to judgment" (223), and her manipulation of the Jew, drawing him deeper and deeper into self-condemnation as she offers him opportunities for the exercise of mercy, wind the comic springs ever tighter. No doubt the scene holds terror as well, and no doubt it generates an almost unbearable suspense; but as those feelings are exacerbated for the onstage audience, they are assuaged for the audience in the theatre and given comic point through Portia's control of pace and nuance. This dual working, in fact, may provide validation in the theatre for both Gratiano's repeated and nearly manic taunting of Shylock and the seeming tendency of audiences to endorse, by their laughter, the young man's outbursts.

In its division into two quite different realms of experience, Venetian mercantilism and the realism of capitalistic venturing on one hand and the romance fairyland of Belmont on the other, *The Merchant of Venice* presents difficulties of interpretation like those posed by the problem plays.[18] The play's fifth act, though it moves to another level and spares only the briefest notice for Shylock, nevertheless continues to employ the theatrical tactic that has been dominant throughout. Here Bassanio and Gratiano, the onstage performers, must improvise roles that will explain or justify the loss of their rings. Rabkin suggests that "Lorenzo's dialogue with Jessica . . . helps both to undercut the enormous emotional claim [Portia] has made on the audience in the trial scene and to call attention to the triviality at best of the game she plays with the ring" (18–19). But is the ring plot trivial? It can be regarded as such, I think, only if we are prepared to ignore one of our most widely shared insights about Shakespeare's method of composition. Characteristically, in plays with double plots—both comedies and tragedies—Shakespeare contrives to have the events involving one set of characters mirror those involving another set.[19] The closing scene of *The Merchant of Venice* brings the play to an end by mirroring the great trial scene. Once again, Portia, assisted by Nerissa, is the judge. As before, she goes about her task with the greatest equanimity, certain of her decision before the examination begins and leading the scene's performers (Bassanio and Gratiano) to a point at which they welcome any gesture of mercy.

If the ring episode concluded only as a trick punctuated by bawdiness (not merely from Gratiano but from Portia and Nerissa as well), a fair judgment would deem it not merely trivial but would see its triviality as diminishing the force of the total play. But the play's close, as it reflects the trial scene, assumes as well some share of that scene's moral weight. Thus, through mirroring, Shakespeare brings together truths about mercy and justice with truths about love and fidelity.

Moreover, he effects this connection by means of a device that dominates the structure of all the major scenes of *The Merchant of Venice*, the tactic of the onstage performer. Here, though, that device is changed as well, for there are two performers—Bassanio and Gratiano. This doubling is a localized instance functioning through character of the mirroring that works through scenes. None of the characters, though Bassanio nearly does, avoids bawdiness altogether; yet it seems a dominant feature of the dialogue between Gratiano and Nerissa and only a slight and indirect element in Portia's speeches. This division of language allows Gratiano to continue his mocking and bumptious ways with talk of "cutler's poetry" and "a little scrubbed boy," with his threat to "mar the young clerk's pen," and with his closing ribaldry:

> Well, while I live I'll fear no other thing
> So sore, as keeping safe Nerissa's ring.
> (306–307)

Over against his insistent loquacity and bawdiness, Shakespeare sets Bassanio, who confesses the loss of his ring only reluctantly and only after Gratiano turns tattletale to justify his own behavior:

> My Lord Bassanio gave his ring away
> Unto the judge that begg'd it, and indeed
> Deserv'd it too; and then the boy, his clerk,
> That took some pains in writing, he begg'd mine,
> And neither man nor master would take aught
> But the two rings.
> (179–84)

The insistent echoing throughout this scene of the word *ring* (it appears no fewer than twenty-two times) may well lead us to attach special significance to it, even to see the rings themselves not as mere symbols of loyalty but to regard them as signifying for the young men something like the equivalent of female virginity. Having given away their rings, Bassanio and Gratiano are judged and judge themselves guilty of betrayal. In some fashion, then, they have diminished their own worth and have done so in a way that identifies them with the female role. Their diminution (in terms of stereotyped sex roles) leads to a corresponding strengthening of Portia and Nerissa, who use their power to generate the rich comedy of the play's closing moments. The pleasure Portia and Nerissa enjoy is like the shared mockery they relish at the expense of the failed suitors. It is even more like the shared assurance they possess as they watch Shylock entrap himself, insisting as he does on the very rigor and precision in the law's operation that will deprive him of his freedom. As we watch the guilty husbands' growing discomfort, and as we admire their wives' growing ingenuity in finding ways of exacerbating that discomfort—"I'll die for't but some woman had the ring!" "I'll have that doctor for [my] bedfellow," "be well advis'd / How you do leave me to mine own protection" (208, 233, 234–35)—our delight in these comic proceedings reflects the delight we felt in those earlier scenes where Portia and Nerissa, as onstage audience, directed and enhanced our perception of onstage performers.

But then Shakespeare executes a major tonal shift as Antonio's interruption—"I am the unhappy subject of these quarrels" (238)—initiates the move to dissolve the performer-spectator relationship on stage and bring all the characters to a condition of equal awareness. Here too there is a reflection of an earlier moment in the play. Bassanio, still ignorant of Portia's ruse, begins a speech that is both plea and pledge:

> Portia, forgive me this enforced wrong,
> And in the hearing of these many friends
> I swear to thee, even by thine own fair eyes,
> Wherein I see myself—
>
> (240–43)

In its unfolding, Bassanio's language recalls that earlier moment when his right choice brought Portia to an experience of pure elation:

> O love, be moderate, allay thy ecstasy,
> In measure rain thy joy, scant this excess!
> I feel too much thy blessing; make it less,
> For fear I surfeit.
>
> (3.2.111–14)

This is not a tone that Shakespeare chooses to sustain as he brings *The Merchant of Venice* to a close. Instead he moves quickly to the revelation by Portia and Nerissa of their scheming, to news of Antonio's argosies, and—most surprisingly—to Gratiano's final naughty quip:

> Well, while I live, I'll fear no other thing
> So sore, as keeping safe Nerissa's ring.

The playwright's reasons for this choice are irrecoverable, and no single critical explanation for his decision is likely to win assent. It may be intended, as John Russell Brown suggests, to make clear to the audience that "Portia and Bassanio are not left on the 'beautiful mountain' in a castle of romance; they are going to live together, like Gratiano and Nerissa, like any two lovers."[20] Whatever the purpose behind it, then, the effect of his comment seems clear: it celebrates joyous life. That note of celebration is the key to the play's final scene: it sounds earlier in Antonio's thanks to Portia—"Sweet lady, you have given me life and living," and in the gratitude of Lorenzo—"Fair ladies, you drop manna in the way / Of starved people" (5.1.286, 294–95).

But this mood of celebration, far from being a new element that emerges from a plot shadowed by sadness and the threat of blood sacrifice, exists in the play from the very beginning and shapes its major episodes. It governs Antonio's decision to support Bassanio's pilgrimage, and it leavens the tension of the casket scenes with Morocco and Arragon. It bursts forth in Portia's elation and in Bassanio's pleasure-filled giddiness when Bassanio chooses the leaden casket:

> Madam, you have bereft me of all words,
> Only my blood speaks to you in my veins,
> And there is such confusion in my powers,
> As after some oration fairly spoke

By a beloved prince, there doth appear
Among the buzzing pleased multitude,
Where every something, being blent together,
Turns to a wild of nothing, save of joy
Express'd and not express'd.

(3.2.175–83)

Even in the trial scene, though its most striking verbal manifestation appears in Gratiano's heartless crowing at Shylock's overthrow, this celebratory tone is pervasive as Portia controls the trial's movement. And it is here that, in the most fundamental way, she wins for Antonio and thus grants him "life and living." The joyousness of *The Merchant of Venice* is not, then, something that emerges only at its close. It is there throughout the play, and it is communicated chiefly through the device of onstage performers acting out their roles before an onstage audience that directs our perception of events.

Nor does the ending of *The Merchant of Venice* function chiefly as a means of delivering the play's meaning. Those critics who aggrandize closure—both those who follow Barber in finding "no other final scene . . . so completely without irony about the joys it celebrates" (187) and those who stress the play's ironies, discovering in the last scene disquieting evidence of similarities between Venice and Belmont—see the comedy's development as essentially teleological, as the working out of a form whose purpose is to lead to an assertion or a demonstration of meaning. But the "meaning" of *The Merchant of Venice* is not an isolable truth enacted in its final scene. If that were the case, we would be faced with a conflict of apparently mutually exclusive meanings, as Norman Rabkin has demonstrated with regard to other matters in the play, i.e., the characterization of Lorenzo and Jessica and the thematic function of music. Rather, the play's close celebrates values that have been advocated through its unfolding and in both its major plots: giving, good judgment, life, and love. The final scene reflects pre-enactments of its major movements and earlier endorsements of the values it celebrates. In that sense, it is not so much a realized purpose (achieved through unstated and somewhat mysterious means—the recovery of Antonio's fortune—or through a trivial deception—Portia's ring trick) as an earned and anticipated fulfillment. It allows us once again to witness relationships and share emotions that we have already experienced and ratified. Its meaning lies not in a theme discovered in tranquil retrospection but in experience as it registers on our pulses.

three

"The Career of . . . Humor"

Comedy's Triumph in Much Ado about Nothing

hakespeare's choice of a title for his comedy of mistaken observations, false and confused reportings, malicious deceptions, and witty role playing seems to imply an attitude toward the events it encompasses. *Much Ado about Nothing* suggests the superiority of retrospection, a comfortable, wholly secure sense that misunderstandings on every level have been clarified and that, in the long run, such disturbances as the play represents count for little over against the achieved wholeness and social order that dominate its conclusion. Critics of the play, especially those who tend to stress closure and to find in the comedies' endings the sources of their meanings, have not uniformly shared its author's apparent insouciance. On one side are those who stress the joyousness of the play's close and find in Benedick's exuberant command "Strike up, pipers!" an appropriate call for "the . . . symbol of happy marriage, the harmony of music and the measured figures of partnership in dance."[1] For such critics, the "ado" of Shakespeare's play is about "something," and that something is finally the triumph of "clarification," as C. L. Barber would have it, or Claudio's release from "his humourous bondage" (Northrop Frye), or, in the analysis of Robert G. Hunter, the audience's need to extend forgiveness to Claudio so that we may join fully in the redemptive experience that the play affords.[2]

On the other side are those critics who find the "ado" of the play credible and disturbing. For them, *Much Ado about Nothing* raises issues in two realms: that of character and that of mode. In this respect, *Much Ado* is like the problem plays, with Claudio an early version of Bertram and Angelo and with the marriage to a disguised Hero seen as an inadequate romantic solution to a problem whose existence is grounded in a convincingly realistic world.[3] Adherents of this latter view may also place the play in relation to Shakespeare's development, seeing it as extending further a realistic strain in comedy attempted first in *The Merchant of Venice*, or as hinting at a darkness to be given more prominence in *Twelfth Night*. Whatever the precise placement they assign to *Much Ado about Nothing*, such critics are guided by a developmental theory of Shakespeare that is in some cases no more subtle than Dowden's. But where his notion of the stages of Shakespeare's career was tied to the playwright's biography, modern critics tend to see them as part of an evolutionary pattern in which Shakespeare gives increasing attention to matters that are troubling, dark, problematic—a pattern, in other words, that shows Shakespeare's growth in terms calculated to appeal to a twentieth-century audience attuned to just such indeterminate and unsettling matters.

This contention between proponents of the festive view of the play and those who find irony, cynicism, darkness, or some other version of problematic qualities in its resolution is not, of course, unique to discussions of *Much Ado about Nothing*. As my earlier remarks have shown, this is a common division of opinion over nearly all the comedies. The curious fact, though, is that such a dispute should persist in nearly unaltered terms over a play that is itself quite unlike the other comedies in its fundamental structure. Nothing seems more surprising in *Shakespeare's Festive Comedy* than Barber's remark explaining his failure to deal directly with this play: "What I would have to say about *Much Ado About Nothing* can largely be inferred from the discussion of the other festive plays" (222). This is surprising, I believe, for two reasons. First, because the play is so rich and appealing in itself: it seems odd that Barber would forgo the opportunity to engage critically with the skirmishes of Beatrice and Benedick or the self-regarding pronouncements of Dogberry. Second—and this is the greatest reason for surprise—because the play is so unlike the other examples of the form that Barber defines with such persuasive clarity: *Much Ado about Nothing* is structurally quite unlike the paradigm of festive comedy.

It seems important to make this point early in discussing *Much Ado about Nothing*, for in many ways the comedy's major pleasures emerge from and are thus dependent upon its subversion of traditional comic form. That form, at least in romantic comedy of the sort usually associated with Shakespeare, involves young lovers determined on a course of behavior that they find impossible to pursue. Obstacles of fortune, parental disapproval, or social convention stand in their way. Negotiating their way around these obstacles—a process that involves escape or escapism or both—the lovers come finally to a solution of their difficulties and gain their objective at last, effecting in the process a change in the social order that the play world represents. This, of course, is Frye's outline; Barber throws primary stress on the broader movements from restriction through release to clarification. Now *Much Ado about Nothing*, in its broad outlines, seems as far as can be from this design. At the opening of the play, the mood is one of anticipation. Don Pedro's force, victorious in the just-concluded "action" and having lost "few of any sort, and none of name" (7), is arriving in Messina. This news, delivered to Leonato, Hero, and Beatrice, is augmented further under the pressure of their questioning. It may be significant, and surely it is so for the tone of this beginning, that this is the only comedy before *All's Well That Ends Well* that opens with two female characters on the stage (and only *A Midsummer Night's Dream* of the other comedies before 1600 has even one female character on stage at its start). In any event, the two figures who emerge from this further account of the battle are Claudio—distinguished by specific recognition from Don Pedro—and Benedick, whose prominence is elicited by Beatrice's questioning and whose "good service" and soldiership, though attested to by the messenger, come after that reporter's more spontaneous testimony that Benedick is "as pleasant as ever he was" (1.1.37–38).

This long opening scene contains far more, of course, including the entrance of the returning soldiers, the first of many memorable encounters between Beatrice and Benedick, Claudio's confession of his love for Hero, and Don Pedro's proposal that he will "fit [Claudio] with the remedy" to win Leonato's daughter. His proposal, in retrospect a bit too patly delivered and unnecessarily indirect in its operation (something like a Rube Goldberg contraption adapted to a problem in human relations), seems at this point in the play unexceptionable:

> Look what will serve is fit: 'tis once, thou lovest
> And I will fit thee with the remedy.
> I know we shall have revelling to-night;
> I will assume thy part in some disguise,
> And tell fair Hero I am Claudio,
> And in her bosom I'll unclasp my heart,
> And take her hearing prisoner with the force
> And strong encounter of my amorous tale;
> Then after to her father will I break,
> And the conclusion is, she shall be thine.
> In practice let us put it presently.
>
> (318–28)

The point, then, is that by the close of the first act, Shakespeare, so far from introducing a dramatic problem, has created an atmosphere dominated by gaiety (perhaps the favorite word of commentators on this play) and undisturbed by either threats or prohibitions. Don John's very presence may of course be vaguely menacing, and his taciturnity in responding to Leonato's welcome—"I thank you: I am not of many words, but I thank you" (157–58)—certainly suggests that he is not fully assimilated into this chatty company. But on the whole such shadows as he casts count for little in the generally sunny environment of the play's beginning.

That brightness, moreover, continues for some time, for nearly one-third of the play's total length, through 2.1. It does not go wholly uninterrupted, however, for the initial scheming of Don John and his crew, designed to persuade Claudio that Don Pedro, betraying him, has wooed Hero for himself, has its temporarily disruptive effect. Yet the movement of this first third of *Much Ado about Nothing* is wholly different from the beginning stages of any of the other major comedies. Those who wish to be married (Hero and Claudio) find the path to that condition remarkably free from the usual impediments. None of the matters that conventionally block young lovers in comedy—arbitrary laws, parental objections, social distinctions—stand in their way. Relatives and friends alike urge them forward and cooperate in their desire. Those who claim to have no wish to marry (Beatrice and Benedick), so far from being allowed the free exercise of their antiromanticism, likewise find the path to matrimony smoothed before them, by friends intent on bringing them together against their will. Here too the chief agent is Don Pedro. Enlisting the aid of Leonato, Claudio, and Hero, he resolves to "undertake one of Hercules' labours, which is to bring Signior Benedick and the Lady Beatrice into a mountain of affection th'one with th'other" (2.1.364–67).

What is one to make of this curious design? Having demonstrated how different it is from that of the other comedies, it seems important to assert that—as design alone—it is not unique in the canon. Paul and Miriam Mueschke pointed out long ago that between *Much Ado about Nothing* and *Othello* there exist "similarities . . . more numerous than those between any other comedy and tragedy in the entire Shakespeare canon." Enumeration of these similarities makes clear how fundamental they are to the plays' designs:

> The exciting force in both plays is an alliance between virtue and valor which the villain intends to destroy by creating an illusion that the heroine is unchaste. In the comedy the first four scenes—in the tragedy the first three scenes—are treated as a prelude to the main action; a prelude in which the villain's initial attempt to create havoc fails. In both plays a strong-willed villain is substituted for the rival lover of the source. In both, the power of insinuation to engender, heighten, and sustain relatively flimsy ocular proof is stressed.[4]

From a certain point of view, one can easily discern the comic potential in the outward events of *Othello*: an insecure villain and his credulous, manipulable sidekick; an irascible father roused from sleep to learn of his daughter's elopement; a January-May marriage. It is less easy to see the potential for darkness in the opening events of *Much Ado*, to find in the play, as the Mueschkes do, a "concern with the fallibility of the senses and the ravages of mortality" and to see it as evoking "the inexpressible about the riddle of existence and the mystery of the human predicament" (56). Rather, the opening events in *Much Ado* produce comic pleasures that will, with slight changes, emerge repeatedly during the play's action, rewarding and reassuring the audience and making the comedy's close a final iteration designed not to suggest dis-ease but to confirm the essential rightness of the spectators' ongoing responses.

Primary among those pleasures are those derived from the skillful use of comic preparation. Before nearly every major event of *Much Ado about Nothing,* and preceding most of its significant comic moments, Shakespeare prepares his audience for what they are about to witness. This technique is fundamental to comedy. It operates, for example, as a major source of success for most popular stand-up comics. We know before Rodney Dangerfield says a word that at some point in his routine he will complain, "I don't get no respect"; and the result is a delighted response from the audience: this is the joke they have waited for. Illustrations are as numerous as the comics themselves: Jack Benny on money (getting and keeping); Johnny Carson's comparatives "It was hot . . . ," "How hot was it?" "It was so hot that . . . " Comic actors have their turns as well, and the audience counts on them. Hamlet complains about this, and the Pistol of Olivier's *Henry V* film shows how such a familiar comic bit might be exploited on the stage. When playwrights choose to develop this technique as a comic resource, they may do so without the benefit of previously established conditioned responses. They build the expectation within the play itself, sketching in a character's oddities or laying out in advance the intended mechanics of a scene.

In *Much Ado about Nothing,* Benedick's introduction affords the first illustration of this tactic. After twenty-seven lines of dialogue between Leonato and the messenger, during which time Hero and Beatrice presumably register to each other and the audience their reaction to the news, Beatrice inquires, "I pray you, is Signior Mountanto return'd from the wars or no?" (1.1.30–31). Why Beatrice should identify Benedick in this way remains unclear, though the usual explanations—"fencer, duellist" (Arden), "from Italian montanto, a fencing term meaning blow or thrust" (Riverside)—seem less than persuasive.[5] But Hero knows full well that "my cousin means Signior Benedick of Padua" (35–36) and Leonato, excusing his niece's mocking, explains to the messenger that "there is a kind of merry war betwixt Signior Benedick and her: they never meet but there's a skirmish of wit between them" (61–64).

Somewhere between Beatrice's account of Benedick as boaster, coward, trencherman, and affliction and the messenger's report of a "good soldier" and one who "hath done good service . . . in these wars" (48–49) exists the Benedick who will emerge later in the play. But for the moment, and for the sake of his audience's immediate pleasure, Shakespeare gives us a Benedick whose entire function is to fulfill the expectations set up for him at this point in the comedy. How completely this is so appears in the fact that it is Leonato, not Beatrice, who first exploits the preparation of the scene's opening section. When Benedick chirps up in response to Leonato's somewhat hackneyed but incongruous joke about his wife's fidelity—Hero's mother "hath many times told" him that he was Hero's father, says Leonato, and Benedick follows this with "Were you in doubt, sir, that you asked her?"—the old man delivers a smart verbal counterblow: "Signior Benedick, no, for you were then a child" (105–108).

But if Leonato's remark is the first to capitalize on Shakespeare's well-prepared expectations about Benedick, it stands as the briefest preliminary to Beatrice's fuller exploitation of the audience's receptivity. As Don Pedro and Leonato "talk aside,"[6] leaving Claudio and Balthazar to amuse themselves, Don John to chafe at the affability that surrounds Leonato's reception of his brother, and Hero to discover her own response to the "young Florentine called Claudio" who "hath borne himself beyond the promise of his age" (10–14), Beatrice throws out one of the surest winning lines Shakespeare ever provided a female comic character.

The energy of that line, its saucy assurance, impels the whole of the Beatrice-Benedick connection and defines its character: "I wonder that you will still be talking, Signior Benedick, nobody marks you" (116–17). With its utterance, we recognize that the preparation for Benedick's entrance was necessarily entrusted to Beatrice; for, however telling Leonato's retort may seem, the quintessential Benedick appears only after he engages fully with "Lady Disdain." Like other great comic pairs, they nourish one another, and it makes little difference whose serve it is in this game of wit. Hal and Falstaff, creations of this same period, function in the same way, striking sparks off one another, energized by their playful antagonism. Shakespeare moves Beatrice and Benedick forward, then, by similar steps. After Claudio's declaration of his love for Hero and Don Pedro's endorsement of that love, Benedick proclaims his attitude toward marriage:

> That a woman conceived me, I thank her; that she brought me up, I likewise give her most humble thanks; but that I will have a rechate winded in my forehead, or hang my bugle in an invisible baldrick, all women shall pardon me. Because I will not do them the wrong to mistrust any, I will do myself the right to trust none; and the fine is (for the which I may go the finer), I will live a bachelor.
>
> (238–46)

In 2.1, Beatrice responds to Leonato's hope that he will see her "one day fitted with a husband." Her answer, which might in some improbable and romantic fiction lead us to expect a magical resolution, the appearance of some ideal creature, is here merely a blunt and equally earthbound parallel to Benedick's rejection of marriage:

> Not till God make men of some other mettle than earth. Would it not grieve a woman to be overmaster'd with a piece of valiant dust? to make an account of her life to a clod of way-ward marl? No, uncle, I'll none. Adam's sons are my brethren, and truly I hold it a sin to match in my kinred.
>
> (59–65)

Only sixty lines intervene before these two figures are brought together in the dance, preceded by three other couples, each of which has a brief moment at center stage, only to move on as directed by Shakespeare's dialogue fitted to the requirements of the music. The earlier couples—Don Pedro and Hero, Balthazar and Margaret, and Antonio and Ursula—define in part the tone of the proceedings and illustrate the comic potential the situation holds. The men are masked and presumably meant to be unrecognizable (although Antonio's "waggling" head gives him away). The women are unmasked. By the time Beatrice and Benedick take the central position, we recognize that this disparity encourages the men to say what they will in the expectation that they cannot be certainly identified (even Antonio claims to be counterfeiting himself). But the women, who can pretend ignorance of their partners' identities, can employ a singular freedom since the males' masks are not only disguises but in another sense traps.[7] The dance episode, then, leads to a confrontation that Shakespeare has prepared for in two ways: by the parallel development of Benedick and Beatrice up to this point and by the exchanges between the previous couples in the dance. The dialogue between Beatrice and Benedick begins as an ongoing conversation. Beatrice presses the question: "Will you not tell me who told you so?" (125); and we quickly learn that her entreaty has been spurred by a reaction to the slanderous assertion "that I was disdainful, and that I had my good wit out of the 'Hundred Merry Tales'" (129–30).

This episode, with its witty energy and improvisational sparkle, stands as something like an epitome of the entire Beatrice-Benedick plot line in *Much Ado about Nothing.* Not only does it give us the characters at the full stretch of their jesting, it reveals them through a situation that pre-enacts their later spying scenes and reveals depths of feeling that will be exhibited further under the pressure of Hero's repudiation. It seems clear that for this scene to work, first Benedick and then Beatrice must claim the advantage of superior knowledge. For Benedick, this is a constant in the scene. He can slander Beatrice freely, attributing his remarks to unidentified other parties while he enjoys her discomfiture from the supposed safety of his disguise. At some point, though, Beatrice sees through that disguise. Just when this happens or how she recognizes her antagonist is unclear from the text. Antonio's disguise proved inadequate to conceal his identity from Ursula; later, Borachio recognizes Claudio "by his bearing" (159–60).

A director would be free to devise some likely means for Beatrice's discovery, but it seems to have taken place before Benedick's first "What's he?" since in the dialogue that follows Beatrice exploits her partner's anxiety about her view of him. Benedick's disguise thus becomes a trap. Having mocked Beatrice with such impunity, he must now suffer her abuse without the chance of a direct reply. Worse yet, since he is unaware that she has penetrated his disguise, he can only assume that Beatrice's remarks have a basis in her honest feelings about him. Benedick is relatively silent, then, as this encounter comes to a close. His engaging to report Beatrice's remarks "when I know the gentleman" (144) and his parting qualification—that they should follow the leaders only "in every good thing" (152)—alike suggest a chastening of his mocker's wit and the presence of sentiments that his literal mask, like the verbal concealment he habitually employs, can but imperfectly conceal. As the dancing comes to a close, the audience is aware that both Beatrice and Benedick are vulnerable to "practice"—i.e., they can be duped—and far more vulnerable than their outward shows would suggest. The spying scenes show them as victims of practice; the chapel scene allows them to express their feelings in a context that demands honesty and fair dealing.

The two spying scenes define in some ways the dominant tone of *Much Ado about Nothing*. Involving a trio of male plotters in the first instance and a more practiced female duo in the second, the scenes mirror one another as they constitute yet another stage in the parallel treatment of Benedick and Beatrice. Together these two scenes convey a sense of a timeless, idle world where courtship and ingenious pranksterism dwell easily, each activity a natural product of youthful high spirits and patrician idleness. The scenes have been treated extensively in previous criticism, and there is no need to rehearse their unfolding here.[8] It may be useful, though, to underline once again their theatrical brilliance and to emphasize a point central to my argument, the position of the victims of deception once their friends have concluded their fooling.

In the first of these scenes, Benedick hides himself in the arbor at the approach of "the Prince and Monsieur Love" (2.3.35–36). They are the chief actors in the little company intent on duping Benedick; the third of their troupe, Leonato, has a significant role but small ability. Like Nathaniel in *Love's Labour's Lost* he is "o'er-parted." At crucial points he seems to lose his place, and the prompting he requires adds a further ingredient—a sort of tension—to a scene already filled with sparkling theatrical effects. But despite Leonato's weakness, the plotters achieve their desired end. Benedick, like Henry V on the night before Agincourt, is a prisoner of his own deception just as he was in the dance scene. He is forced to hear criticism of himself without any prospect of offering a refutation. But more significant here, that criticism is balanced by news of Beatrice's love for him, a love which is the product of "wisdom and blood combating in so tender a body." Having heard of her affection, Benedick illustrates once again that in such a struggle "we have ten proofs to one that blood hath the victory" (163–65).

Benedick's triumphant conclusion—"No, the world must be peopled" (242)—is more than just his reflection of what he has overheard. After the plotters depart, he comes forward to address the audience directly. In the theatre, the resulting engagement generates extraordinary emotional power. When Bottom awakens from his sleep in *A Midsummer Night's Dream,* he turns to the audience in a similar fashion. "I have had," he declares, "a most rare vision" (4.1.204–205); and the rest of his speech, in which feelings of excited wonder overwhelm his verbal capacity, brings elation to the point of joyous tears. Here, Benedick's speech generates something like the same effect. He begins as well with an appeal to the validity of his experience: "This," he asserts, "can be no trick" (220). Then, having persuaded himself of the truth of what he has just heard, he propels himself, with a barely controllable joy, toward the resolution that such a judgment seems to demand. The procreative imperative that Benedick lights on emerges from a speech that nearly explodes with energy.

> I hear how I am censur'd; they say I will bear myself proudly, if I perceive the love come from her; they say too that she will rather die than give any sign of affection. I did never think to marry. I must not seem proud; happy are they that can hear their detractions, and can put them to mending. . . . Shall quips and sentences and these paper bullets of the brain awe a man from the career of his humor?
>
> (224–30, 240–42)

He is not yet "Benedick the married man," but his every word testifies to the joy he anticipates in that status.

Benedick, cocksure but teachable, participates in his own gulling: "This can be no trick" (220). Beatrice, equally fooled, responds more bemusedly: "Can this be true?" (3.1.107). Again, Shakespeare brings the two characters forward in tandem. Like Benedick, Beatrice condemns her earlier behavior and resolves to abandon it. Like him, she too proclaims her transformation to the audience. Once again the spectators of *Much Ado about Nothing* find themselves the sole witnesses to a remarkable metamorphosis. "My Lady Tongue," renouncing "contempt" and "maiden pride," joyfully pledges herself to the man who has been the object of her unremitting scorn:

> Benedick, love on, I will requite thee,
> Taming my wild heart to thy loving hand.

> If thou dost love, my kindness shall incite thee
> To bind our loves up in a holy band;
> For others say thou dost deserve, and I
> Believe it better than reportingly.
>
> (3.1.111–16)

In witnessing both conversions, the audience is especially privileged. In the initial spying scene involving Benedick, Don Pedro, Claudio, and Leonato exit, leaving the stage to their dupe, to whom they plan to "send [Beatrice] to call him in to dinner" (218–19). Thus they miss one side of the very encounter that their contrivance is designed to produce. "The sport will be," says Don Pedro, relishing the brilliance of his plot, "when they hold one an opinion of the other's dotage, and no such matter; that's the scene that I would see, which will be merely a dumb show" (215–18). Similarly, in the spying scene in which Ursula and Hero delude Beatrice, the two women leave without reaping the full benefit of their play-acting. Although Ursula is persuaded that the ruse has worked—"She's limed, I warrant you. We have caught her, madam" (103)—Hero's conditional response is more cautiously optimistic:

> If it prove so, then loving goes by haps:
> Some Cupid kills with arrows, some with traps.
>
> (105–106)

Shakespeare then gives the theatre audience full confirmation that Hero and Ursula have succeeded in their devising of "little Cupid's crafty arrow." Although their "angling" for Beatrice—to shift metaphors along with Shakespeare—is successful, they do not remain on stage to enjoy "the pleasant'st angling,"

> to see the fish
> Cut with her golden oars the silver stream,
> And greedily devour the treacherous bait.
>
> (26–28)

That pleasure is left for the spectators in the theatre, who at this point, less than halfway through the play, not only witness the elation that Beatrice and Benedick feel but participate in it as well.

The spying scenes, then, function as pre-enactments of the play's close, at least of that part of its ending focused on Beatrice and Benedick. In the first of them, Benedick's gulling is preceded by a song. Before Balthazar's performance, the musician disparages his own musical talents. Yet his auditors apparently find his efforts moving enough to excite Benedick's scorn: "Now, divine air! now his soul is ravish'd! Is it not strange that sheep's guts should hale souls out of men's bodies?" (58–60).[9] Then, after Balthazar sings "Sigh no more, ladies," Benedick remains adamantly critical: "I had as live have heard the night-raven, come what plague could have come after it" (81–83). But surely Benedick, even in concealment, is remaining true to his public character. In the total economy of the scene, Balthazar's song functions like Feste's performance in *Twelfth Night* 2.4 or like the song that accompanies Bassanio's choice in the casket scene (3.2). It works on the spectators, encouraging in each case a receptive mood toward the scene's tonal outcome, preparing them for Portia's access of emotion ("O love be moderate, allay thy ecstasy"), for Viola's nearly reverent echo of Orsino's sentimentalism ("It gives a very echo to the seat where love is thron'd"), and for Benedick's joyous conversion ("When I said I would die a bachelor, I did not think I should live till I were married" [2.3.242–44]).

Beatrice's transformation goes forward unaccompanied by music, but the shift to blank verse in 3.1 has an effect similar to that of the music Shakespeare employs in the earlier scene.[10] While the male tricksters improvise and adjust their performance to accommodate Leonato's inadequacies, Hero and Ursula perform in a virtuoso fashion, matching one another perfectly and offering a beautifully modulated variety of verbal styles. Hero's near-aria on Beatrice's pride has a passionate clarity that looks forward to Viola's complexly motivated address to Olivia ("If I did love you in my master's flame" [1.5.264]):

> O god of love! I know he doth deserve
> As much as may be yielded to a man;
> But nature never fram'd a woman's heart
> Of prouder stuff than that of Beatrice.
> Disdain and scorn ride sparkling in her eyes,
> Misprising what they look on, and her wit
> Values itself so highly that to her
> All matter else seems weak. She cannot love,

> Nor take no shape nor project of affection,
> She is so self-endeared.
>
> (47–56)

Hero moves from this lament over Beatrice's haughtiness to a crisp parody of her cousin's style of mocking:

> I never yet saw man,
> How wise, how noble, young, how rarely featur'd,
> But she would spell him backward. If fair-fac'd,
> She would swear the gentleman should be her sister;
> If black, why, Nature, drawing of an antic,
> Made a foul blot; if tall, a lance ill-headed;
> If low, an agot very vildly cut;
> If speaking, why, a vane blown with all winds;
> If silent, why, a block moved with none.
>
> (59–67)

The conclusion of this gulling dialogue is a kind of responsive litany of praise for Benedick: "so rare a gentleman," "the only man of Italy," "for shape, for bearing, argument, and valor . . . foremost in report," "an excellent good name" (91–98). Beatrice witnesses this wonderfully varied performance in silence, coming forward after the departure of Hero and Ursula not merely to announce her resolve to change—"Contempt, farewell, and maiden pride, adieu!" (109)—but revealing the suddenness of that transition in accents that resonate for her and for the theatre audience with surprising emotion: "Benedick, love on, I will requite thee, / Taming my wild heart to thy loving hand" (111–12).

After this point, the Benedick-Beatrice plot merges with the Hero-Claudio line of action, although the former antagonists are alone among the play's principal characters in being personally untouched by Don John's villainy. The scene that Don Pedro "would see, which will be merely a dumb show" (2.3.217–18), takes place in the chapel in 4.1 after Hero's public disgrace. Far from being a dumb show, it contains the most direct and earnest dialogue given these characters in the course of the entire play. Shadowed by the ugliness of Claudio's behavior and impelled by concern for Hero, the speeches of Beatrice and Benedick have an urgency that allows neither coyness nor protective mockery. The famous injunction "Kill

Claudio," startling and even comic as it may sometimes seem, grows naturally out of the immediate dramatic circumstances and out of the characters' understanding of one another. No matter that the understanding has been freed by deception; the spying scenes created no new attitudes, they merely brought to the surface affections and the potential for feeling that had been covered over by a veneer of witty disregard. For Benedick, "Kill Claudio" is the equivalent of Bassanio's casket scene. It provides an occasion for him to "give and hazard all he hath." Despite his initial and understandable reluctance, he moves by the scene's close to obey Beatrice's demands and the claims of love, recognizing in them a stronger force than those exerted on behalf of Claudio and the bonds of friendship.

Here, then, and throughout the rest of the play, Beatrice and Benedick do nothing to surprise the theatre audience. The terms of their love, ratified at the close of the spying scenes, are pledged in unison and with entire appropriateness in the chapel. Other characters in the play may enjoy further mirth at their expense, as in the ill-timed mockery of Claudio and Don Pedro (5.1.159–84), and the lovers themselves may lapse into old habits (5.2.42–94); but the anticipation of the play's final tone at the close of the spying scenes and its enhancement in the chapel scene allow us as spectators one further fulfillment of pleasurable anticipation, the point at which Benedick, employing a sure means of silencing the voluble wit of Lady Tongue, takes Beatrice in his arms and kisses her: "Peace, I will stop your mouth" (5.4.97).

Thus closure in *Much Ado about Nothing*, as it relates to the Beatrice-Benedick line of action, neither affects transformations nor delivers final meanings. It re-enacts for the play's other characters attitudes and feelings that the theatre audience has already witnessed and experienced. But despite the early recognition that the witty lovers offer greater theatrical rewards than their quieter and more somber counterparts—Charles I, in his copy of the second folio, labeled the play "Benedict and Betteris"[11]—most of the issues surrounding the close of *Much Ado*, and certainly the chief features that for many critics render it problematic, are tied up with the Hero-Claudio plot. That plot—from its initial confusion over Don Pedro's role as surrogate suitor, through Don John's deception; Claudio's disgracing of Hero "in the congregation where [he] should wed" (3.2.124–25); Don Pedro's encounters with Antonio and Leonato, then with Benedick; the statue scene; and the wedding ceremony that unites the restored Hero and her lover—seems overburdened with matters that afford no comic resolution. Thus when closure finally does occur, Claudio remains for many critics outside the circle of affectionate regard established by Benedick in the dance that brings the play to an end. Claudio, in his defensiveness—"yet sinn'd I not / But in mistaking" (5.1.273–74)—seems to many critics no more agreeable than Bertram, whose acceptance of Helena in *All's Well That Ends Well* sounds grudgingly conditional: "If she, my liege, can make me know this clearly, / I'll love her dearly, ever, ever dearly" (5.3.315–16).

It may be helpful to begin an investigation of this second line of action at the point of its resolution. The play's final scene is divided rather neatly into two parts. The first of these ends with the revelation to Claudio, prepared to wed Antonio's daughter, that he instead will be joined to "the former Hero! Hero that is dead!" who "died . . . but whiles her slander liv'd" (5.4.65–66). Friar Francis then provides a bridge to the scene's second half:

> All this amazement can I qualify,
> When after that the holy rites are ended,
> I'll tell you largely of fair Hero's death.
> Mean time let wonder seem familiar,
> And to the chapel let us presently.
> (67–71)

From this point on through Benedick's insistence that dancing precede the wedding ceremony and his closing assertion of his will—"Strike up pipers!"—the scene belongs to Benedick and Beatrice. There are, I think, two matters worth remarking about Shakespeare's dramatic tactics at this point in the play. First, everything from line 72 (Benedick's "Soft and fair, Friar, which is Beatrice?") to line 98 ("Peace, I will stop your mouth") is in the nature of a reprise. The revelation of the sonnets—"A miracle!" marvels Benedick—is no miracle to him at all but further and welcome support for what seems to the other characters an act of capitulation but to the theatre audience an anticipated and relished outcome. Second, Benedick uses the security of his love for Beatrice as the basis for his control of the play's closing moments, the last quarter of the final scene. Inferior in rank to Don Pedro, Leonato's guest and an outsider in Messina, Benedick nevertheless directs the play to its end, putting down the prince, overruling Leonato, and taking it upon himself to "devise . . . brave punishments" for Don John, whose case he defers until the morrow.[12]

The chief effect of Benedick's domination of this final scene is to throw the "problem" of Hero and Claudio (indeed, to place their whole relationship) into a decidedly secondary position. Benedick in this final scene is once again "as pleasant as ever he was," and his character controls the tone of the play's ending. That tone is not new, of course, as my earlier remarks on its pre-enactments establish; it is, however, worth observing here its effect on the second love plot. But there are other matters as well that condition our view of Claudio and Hero at this point. One of these is the staging of the final scene as the ladies arrive superintended by Antonio, in masks. Inevitably, their appearance recalls the dance of 2.1, though with the difference that on that occasion the men, rather than the women, wore masks. Apart from a pleasing but rather simple symmetry, this masking seems to introduce a note that Shakespeare recurs to again and again when his interest focuses on ideas of redemption and forgiveness. "Let wonder seem familiar," says Friar Francis, urging Claudio and Don Pedro to oxymoronic credulity. Such a belief can be achieved only through an effort of will, for *wonder*, a word at home in the realm of the romances, seems out of place in the realistic world of *Much Ado about Nothing*.[13] Yet it appears that the effort to make "wonder seem familiar" is at the center of Shakespeare's design in this play and the key to his management of the Hero-Claudio plot.

In Shakespeare's other love comedies, one often finds a contrast between two worlds of love—a rarefied, idealized world that nourishes itself on elegant language, and a world focused on physical attractiveness and the appeal of the body. It is as though Shakespeare uses the second world to supply a deficiency in the first or—more precisely—as though he wants to provide the first with an element it lacks while keeping its generally lofty tone free from any immediate taint. As with other forms of mirroring in Shakespeare, the efforts move in two directions so that the two worlds complement one another, each supplying, as our imagination assists their interpenetration, the dimension missing in the other. So in *Twelfth Night* Orsino has "unclasp'd / . . . the book even of [his] secret soul," while Feste avers to Maria that, "if ever Sir Toby would leave drinking thou wert as witty a piece of Eve's flesh as any in Illyria" (1.4.13–14; 1.5.27–28). Thus Orlando in *As You Like It* exercises his passion in idealizing but rather feeble poetry:

> Thus Rosalind of many parts
> By heavenly synod was devis'd,
> Of many faces, eyes, and hearts,
> To have the touches dearest priz'd.
> (3.2.149–52)

while Touchstone presses in "amongst the rest of the country copulatives" (5.4.55–56).

In *Much Ado about Nothing*, this complementary relationship looks to be available in the balance between the two pairs of lovers. Benedick and Beatrice, for their part, supply bountiful reminders of the physical basis of love. Whether rejecting love or accepting it, Beatrice speaks the language of the body. "Would it not grieve a woman," she asks, "to be overmaster'd with a piece of valiant dust? to make an account of her life to a piece of wayward marl?" (2.1.60–63). And in response to Pedro's comment on her victory over Benedick—"You have put him down, lady, you have put him down"—she replies, "So would I not he should do me, my lord, lest I should prove to be the mother of fools" (2.1.283–86). Benedick, with his nearly compulsive talk of horns and cuckoldry, reinforces this emphasis on sex and the physical nature of love. Moreover, he explicitly rejects the behavior of others, those who illustrate the "shallow follies" typically associated with young men in love.

But the other side of this contrast between two views of love is simply not supported adequately by Hero and Claudio. True, Benedick cites his comrade as an example of one who has "become the argument of his own scorn by falling in love" (2.3.10–11). Claudio now prefers "the tabor and pipe" to "the drum and the fife"; he "now will . . . lie ten nights awake carving the fashion of a new doublet"; and rather than "speak plain and to the purpose" he is "turn'd orthography—his words are a very fantastical banquet, just so many strange dishes" (2.3.13–21). But this vivid description is mirrored in neither the language nor the behavior of Claudio. Hero, whose salient characteristics are her youth, her silence, and her diminutiveness (she is "Leonato's short daughter"), similarly does little to establish in *Much Ado about Nothing* the contrast between two views of love that is such a prominent feature of the other love comedies. Moreover, we see little of Hero and Claudio in the course of the play and far less of the two of them together. They are with one another in 1.1, though without any indication of their behavior toward one another. Presumably, they have a sufficiently meaningful silent exchange during the time Benedick and Beatrice hold the floor (116–45) to provide a credible basis for Claudio's interested question: "Benedick, didst thou notice the daughter of Signior Leonato?" (162–63).

During the dance, however, Shakespeare keeps them apart in order to further the initial "noting" of the play, Claudio's belief that Don Pedro has courted Hero for himself. When that false suspicion is corrected, and Hero and Claudio are brought together (at 2.1.218–301), Beatrice's urging ("Speak, Count, 'tis your cue," "Speak, cousin" [305, 310]) produces little more than Claudio's brief justification for not responding: "Silence is the perfectest heralt of joy; I were but little happy, if I could say how much! Lady, as you are mine, I am yours. I give away myself for you, and dote upon the exchange" (306–309). The couple remains on stage with Don Pedro and Leonato after Beatrice's departure, chiefly to allow Pedro to initiate his gulling plot and win their support in the effort to bring Beatrice and Benedick together: "If we can do this, Cupid is no longer an archer; his glory shall be ours, for we are the only love-gods. Go in with me, and I will tell you my drift" (384–87).

After this point, Hero and Claudio do not appear together on stage until the beginning of 4.1; that is 876 lines, or very nearly one-third of the play's total length. That meeting explodes in the rage of Claudio's repudiation speech:

> There, Leonato, take her back again.
> Give not this rotten orange to your friend,
> She's but the sign and semblance of her honor.
> Behold how like a maid she blushes here.
> O, what authority and show of truth

> Can cunning sin cover itself withal!
> Comes not that blood as modest evidence
> To witness simple virtue? Would you not swear,
> All you that see her, that she were a maid,
> By these exterior shows? But she is none:
> She knows the heat of a luxurious bed;
> Her blush is guiltiness, not modesty.
>
> (31–42)

Their reconciliation in 5.4, marked on Claudio's part only by the amazed "Another Hero!" is cut short by the Friar's haste to perform the "holy rites" (he is perhaps eager to avoid another scene like that in the church) and by Benedick's assumption of control in the play's final moments.

Understood in this way, the Hero-Claudio plot becomes less important than it appears in most readings of *Much Ado about Nothing.* Certainly it does not generate the kind of power to dominate the play's tone, to lend to the whole a sense of tragedy, or to make the play, in John Crick's words, a study of "the power of evil that exists in people who have become self-regarding by living in a society that is closely-knit and turned in on itself."[14]

Why, then, should this line of action, whose principals appear so sketchily in Shakespeare's play, attract such attention? And why should these rather insubstantial characters be seen as posing the chief critical issues of the work and thus, in the view of many critics, as rendering its conclusion dark, unsettling, problematic? The answer, I believe, lies in the origins of *Much Ado about Nothing* and in the peculiar quality of the play itself. The second of these matters needs to be addressed first. I spoke before of the "gaiety" of *Much Ado* and of the popularity of that term with its commentators. Other distinguishing characteristics of the comedy are its realism and solidity, the clarity of its prose, its wonderfully managed wit combats, and a structure that is effectively articulated and straightforward. But these qualities, engaging as they are, have a common drawback. They do not invite extensive critical discussion. Messina is Messina, a substantial Italian city which serves as a retreat for victorious soldiers and which just happens to enjoy the services of a thoroughly English constable named Dogberry. There is no Belmont nearby, nor even a convenient wood or forest. Benedick and Beatrice make a brilliant pair, but we always know who they are. Beatrice may disguise her love but not her person: no Ganymed instructs Benedick, though he—like Orlando—is a failed verse maker; and no melancholy page longs to tell a master of her love. This, I suspect, is what kept C. L. Barber from treating *Much Ado about Nothing*. The play is, quite simply, resistant to the forms of critical discourse most frequently employed in the discussion of Shakespeare's comedies.

But while *Much Ado about Nothing* as Shakespeare has given it to us may inhibit discussion, his procedures and tactical judgments in creating the play from its sources provide an inviting field for critical speculation and analysis.[15] The one substantial book devoted exclusively to the play is Charles T. Prouty's study *The Sources of* Much Ado about Nothing, actually a short (sixty-four pages) monograph with which is printed Peter Beverly's *Ariodanto and Ieneura*, one of the several sources for the plot involving Hero and Claudio. Prouty's argument, at the most general level, makes a claim for unity in the play's design, a unity of purpose that he sees as determining Shakespeare's choices among the sources of the Hero-Claudio story and influencing the playwright's emphasis on the antiromantic, realistic elements in the Beatrice-Benedick plot. In this view, Claudio and Hero, a businesslike young man and an obedient daughter, contract for a *mariage de convenance*, a business arrangement that seems to preclude any concern with romantic love. Similarly, Benedick and Beatrice, though motivated by love, seek to "avoid the folly which they both see in the trite and conventional" behavior of literary lovers.[16] Although Prouty confuses art and life somewhat in this discussion, seeing one pair of lovers as realistic because they adhere to a common social practice and the other pair as realistic because they avoid the behavior of other figures in literature, his main point is clear. *Much Ado about Nothing*, Shakespeare's "reaction to the ideas and characters of his sources" (46), is a play about love and marriage that rejects the romantic tradition and embraces realism.

It seems worth noting that such a view of Shakespeare's play produces rather flat critical results, as when Prouty makes the following claim:

> Viewed as a *mariage de convenance*, the projected alliance and its breach demand another standard of judgment than that of romantic

> love. The public denunciation of Hero is an unpleasant affair, but Pedro and Claudio are more than justified, since they accept for truth the evidence which they have seen.
>
> (46)

But the chief point that Prouty's book illustrates is something quite different, and that is the control exerted over discussions of *Much Ado about Nothing* by concentration on the Hero-Claudio plot, a control grounded primarily on that plot's sources. In Prouty's interpretation, for example, Shakespeare arrived at his treatment of the play's main story by a judicious process of selection from among its various antecedents. Then, having settled on his management of that story, he designed the characters of Benedick and Beatrice (whose sources are not to be discovered in any plot as such, but in similar pairs of witty antagonists or simply in single love cynics of either sex) to complement the thematic and aesthetic choices he had already made.

The nature of Prouty's enterprise almost necessitates the kind of imbalance I have just described. He is, after all, involved in a study of sources, and the likely sources for one set of lovers are both more numerous and more detailed than the sources for the other pair. But the assumption behind his procedure controls much of the criticism of *Much Ado about Nothing*, including many studies of the play quite different from Prouty's in method and focus. How easily this happens may be seen in Anne Barton's introduction to the play in *The Riverside Shakespeare*. Having noted the great antiquity of the Hero-Claudio plot and its wide popularity during the Renaissance, she turns to the versions of the story likely to have influenced the composition of *Much Ado*:

> In constructing his own version of this archetypal story of the lady falsely accused of unchastity, cast off by her lover, and after many vicissitudes restored to him again, Shakespeare probably had at least four non-dramatic variants of the tale somewhere in mind.[17]

It seems fair to say that this is not quite an accurate summary of Shakespeare's "own version" of a familiar story, chiefly because the "vicissitudes," which may bulk large in other versions, are here almost totally absent. Apart from the discrepancy between the Friar's sanguine expectations and what actually occurs—i.e., he believes that "th' idea of [Hero's] life" will so overwhelm Claudio that he shall "mourn, / . . . And wish he had not so accus'd her; / No, though he thought his accusation true" (4.1.224, 230–33), whereas Claudio agrees to honor Hero and marry her cousin only after he learns of her innocence—no changes of fortune touch Hero at all. But knowledge of the story's sources and their relative complexity seems to have colored Barton's account, despite her belief that "Shakespeare cannot have been unaware of the disproportionate amount of interest generated by the subplot" (327). Even her reference to a "subplot" in this instance seems to misrepresent the case.

Such tacit granting of primacy to the Hero-Claudio story is the nearly invariable basis for views of the play that stress its darkness or its problematic nature. Thus Furness objects to the way Shakespeare brings *Much Ado* to a close:

> This is the only play of Shakespeare thus ending with a "Dance," and I cannot but regret that the rule is here broken. Although the atmosphere is now all gaiety and happiness, we cannot forget how heavily charged it was, only a few hours before, with tragedy.
>
> (287)

A. R. Humphreys, the Arden editor of *Much Ado about Nothing*, sees Shakespeare's construction of the play as a process of "interweaving Bandello's materials with Ariosto's" and from "elements loosely similar but . . . markedly variant in tone and incidents" shaping "a theme of . . . tragicomic force" (12–13). He goes on to point out how "Beatrice, Benedick, and Dogberry affect the tenor of the serious plot throughout"; but the Hero-Claudio story gets top billing, and their prominence somehow enables Humphreys to speak of the church scene as "so startling that the inmost natures of the participants disclose themselves in a way alien to mere comedy" (12).

Joseph A. Bryant, Jr., is insistent that the "merry war" of the play is a subordinate element:

> The Roman or New Comedy plot—the marketing of a marriageable daughter—is actually, not just nominally, the ground of the action. Regardless of what producers and critics have done with it down through the centuries, *Much Ado* properly belongs to Claudio, Hero, Don Pedro, Leonato, and company rather than to Benedick and Beatrice.[18]

By thus asserting the dominance of the Hero-Claudio action, Bryant opens the way to his description of "the artificiality of Messina's courtly society, in which sophisticated people live and love and sometimes die by a code that has long since ceased to define any of the realities of human life." Moreover, the view that "Messina, at the level that preoccupies us in the play is a loveless society," a view that minimizes the importance of Benedick and Beatrice, enables him to regard Don John and Beatrice as outsiders whose treatment in the play teaches us that "the unenfranchised—among them bastards and orphans and, in general, women—will do well to live and die inconspicuously" (128, 132–33).

This concern for Don John seems so misplaced that it nearly tempts one, against every good instinct, to revive the term *bleeding heart;* perhaps Bryant, moved by Edmund's injunction "Now, gods, stand up for bastards," has merely decided to join in supporting society's underdogs. But the displacement of Beatrice is the key matter here, the tactic that allows Bryant to illustrate the emergence of the play's meaning in its close. And it is the initial stage of his argument—the claim that "the ground of the action" in *Much Ado* is to be discovered in the story of Hero and Claudio—that permits him to assign Beatrice a subordinate position along with Don Pedro's laconic, villainous bastard brother, a most improbable companion for Lady Tongue.

In 1979, M. M. Mahood summed up a generation of criticism of the middle comedies—*As You Like It, Much Ado about Nothing,* and *Twelfth Night.* Her rather brisk account of the critical fortunes of *Much Ado* seems instructive both for its own lively wit and for its implied sense of the play and its merits. She writes, for example, of Claudio's being subjected by the critics to "a whole thesaurus of abuse" and then goes on to record over thirty terms of opprobrium used to describe him.[19] More important, she acknowledges the play's unusual and confusing structure without wishing it to be other than it is or searching for a single interpretive notion that would demonstrate its unity. Finding in it something like the qualities of a maze, she suggests that it seems wrong-headed to ask for a map of its surprising turns and indirections. To that view, I would add that critical maps are too often concerned with destinations, with the journey's end. They serve as solutions to a puzzle rather than guides to the enjoyment of the travel itself.

In *Much Ado about Nothing,* the route that leads to Benedick's "Strike up, pipers!" affords a great many comic pleasures, some of which anticipate and even pre-enact the eventual union of Benedick and Beatrice. Claudio and Hero have a bumpier road to happiness, but Shakespeare diminishes their functions in the play's overall design so that their story, ostensibly the main plot, becomes the occasion for his comic invention rather than the comedy's central and tonally dominant concern. Moreover, as Bertrand Evans has demonstrated, the playwright's use of discrepant awareness provides his audience with a comic guarantee, early assurance that the scheme designed "to misuse the Prince, to vex Claudio, to undo Hero, and kill Leonato" (2.2.38–40) has been discovered and faces imminent exposure. *Imminent* may be a relative term, given that the discovery must first be communicated by the watch to Dogberry and then, by him, to someone capable of acting on the information. But placing this responsibility on Dogberry, far from threatening the play's comic tone, enhances it.

The "near-tragic" plot of *Much Ado,* seen in this way, looks a good deal less threatening and causes no major disruption of the play's predominantly comic tone. Like Abbott and Costello on the trail of jewel thieves or Peter Sellers in pursuit of some ingenious spy, the comic forces of justice in *Much Ado about Nothing* bring the play's villainy into their orbit. Shakespeare reinforces this effect in the structuring of events surrounding the deception and its discovery. Having set the trap in 3.2, Don John urges Don Pedro and Claudio to "bear it coldly but till midnight, and let the issue show itself" (129–30). Their responses, capped by Don John's echo, lend themselves to a comic reading, much like Hermia's interruptions of Lysander's "course of true love" speech in *A Midsummer Night's Dream* (1.1.136–40):

D. Pedro. O day untowardly turn'd!
Claud. O mischief strangely thwarting!
D. John. O plague right well prevented! So will you say when you have seen the sequel.

(131–34)

This moment leads directly to the first appearance of Dogberry and Verges, the charge to the Watch, and the determination of those "good men and true" to "sit here upon the church-bench till two, and then all to bed" (89–90). At the exit of Dogberry and Verges, Borachio and Conrad enter and—fewer than one hundred lines later—fall into the hands of the Watch. Thus Borachio hardly has time to leave the scene of his infamous deception before his own drunken garrulity undoes him. It seems important to note that this entire plot against the young lovers was of Borachio's devising and not, in its inception, a scheme invented by Don John. Thus the principal source of darkness in *Much Ado about Nothing,* generated by a comic underling and kept deliberately from the audience's view, has only the briefest existence free from discovery and is brought to light (under a penthouse, in a drizzling rain) in circumstances guaranteed to ensure that it will be viewed in a comic perspective.

Earlier in this discussion, I spoke about the realism of *Much Ado about Nothing* and about the ways in which the qualities of the play related to its realism tended to inhibit critical discourse about it. Perhaps this is what A. P. Rossiter means when he points to the play's "bright hardness," its "*Decameron* qualities of volatility in the persons, no wasting of sympathy on victims of jests, and the expectation of swift, unreflecting volte-faces of attitudes and emotions at the call of Fortune's pipe."[20]

Dogberry offers a striking instance of this resistance to criticism. Set beside any of the other great clown figures in the Shakespeare canon, Dogberry seems another breed altogether. He shares Bottom's linguistic ineptitude and something of his pushiness, but nothing of the weaver's pathos. Like Feste, he has knowledge unavailable to others, but nothing of the clown's wit. Even when he is compared with Launcelot Gobbo, we notice Dogberry's deficiencies and find it hard to say more about him than that "in the theatre" he more than earns his way. Moreover, with each of the other characters one can find good arguments for judging the clown's performance to be integral to the play's thematic design. In Dogberry's case, the idea of "noting" joins him to the play's other plot elements; but this seems rather a matter of unity of plot than an example of thematic coherence.

Borachio, confessing to Don Pedro his part in the deception, tells the Prince, "What your wisdoms could not discover, these shallow fools have brought to light" (5.1.232–34). But Dogberry leaves the stage without witnessing the outcome of his discovery: the revelation of the restored Hero and the movement to marriage signaled by the play's final dance. His role in the play has been chiefly a matter of providing a certain sure-fire comic pleasure. As he exits for the last time in 5.1, his need to talk, to be recognized, threatens to keep him on stage. Leonato, civil but emphatic, urges his departure: "I thank thee for thy care and honest pains"; "There's for thy pains"; "Go, I discharge thee of thy prisoner, and I thank thee" (314, 317, 319–20). Here, unlike in 3.5, where we regretted Leonato's impatience with folly and wished that Dogberry might get to the point, we realize that for the constable there is no point. He is the master of much ado about nothing: "God keep your worship! I wish your worship well. I humbly give you leave to depart, and if a merry meeting may be wish'd, God prohibit it" (323–26).

Of all Shakespeare's comedies, *Much Ado about Nothing* seems most uncongenial to interpretations that look for meaning to emerge at the point of closure. Its clown exits having discharged his plot function as a representative of the legal system, leaving the administration of justice to his betters. At his departure, he urges only that "it be remember'd" that "this plaintiff here, the offender, did call me ass" and that Leonato be alert to the threat to civil rule posed by "one Deform'd" (5.1.304–308). The chief victims of the scheme so easily brought to light, Hero and Claudio, suffer no irreparable harm from the slander that brought her to disgrace and exposed in him a sexual revulsion rooted in insecurity. He takes her hand while she is still masked, believing her to be Antonio's daughter:

> Give me your hand before this holy friar—
> I am your husband if you like of me.

and remains in that posture as Hero declares her identity:

> And when I liv'd I was your other wife,
> And when you lov'd, you were my other husband.
> (5.4.58–61)

They take up their love with a gesture that seems continuous with their first pledge, and so little concerned is Shakespeare at this point with questions of character and identity that his young lovers might adopt as their shared motto Claudio's earlier statement of commitment: "I give away myself for you, and dote upon the exchange" (2.1.308–309).

Benedick and Beatrice, won to each other's love in the spying episodes and confirmed in their "mountain of affection" at the close of the chapel scene, re-enact their understanding in the comic vein that still serves them for public occasions, thus giving Don Pedro one last opportunity for mockery. But Benedick now has the final word: "Since I do purpose to marry, I will think nothing to any purpose that the world can say against it; for man is a giddy thing, and this is my conclusion" (5.4.105–109). Benedick's "conclusion" involves the slightest but most telling ambiguity. He concludes *as* "Benedick the married man," but he concludes *that* "man is a giddy thing." This latter insight is no revelation to the audience of *Much Ado about Nothing*. From the initial misconception about Don Pedro's intentions towards Hero, through the mistakings at the dance, the spying scenes, and Claudio's precipitous rejection of his intended bride, giddiness marks the entire action of the play. Like the ending of the comedy itself, Benedick's "conclusion" merely reasserts what our total experience of *Much Ado about Nothing* leads us to know.

Performative Comedy in *As You Like It*

n the preceding discussions I have argued that an emphasis on closure has been imposed upon certain of Shakespeare's comedies and that the Procrustean tendencies of such criticism have shaped (or misshaped) the plays in ways that have left them not merely distorted but, at times, distinctly uncomic. I do not wish to abandon that argument in discussing *As You Like It*. Still, it would seem disingenuous to suggest that the play itself does not encourage such an emphasis. More fully, perhaps, than any other comedy in the Shakespeare canon, *As You Like It* draws special attention to its close. It does so in part because of its overall design; but, more particularly, it does so because as it moves to an ending it makes use of a variety of special features that call attention to themselves through their rarity, the unusual means of their employment, or both.

The briefest recapitulation of the dominant structure of the comedies, a central feature of what I have called the Barber-Frye line of criticism, makes evident how paradigmatic a case *As You Like It* provides. The movement from a corrupt and rule-ridden world governed by an essentially unsympathetic older generation, a period of license and release in a setting that symbolizes and thus encourages free play, a return to the reality of proper social relations (now changed, and redefined by the claims of the younger characters): all these elements make up the context of a well-rehearsed critical formulation. From one point of view, *As You Like It* does not merely fit the Barber-Frye pattern, it defines that pattern. Approaching the play with Barber and Frye and their numerous followers to guide us, we are in familiar territory and know far more of what the location implies than Rosalind can imagine when she says, "Well, this is the forest of Arden" (2.4.15).

This familiar comic design, which in itself throws considerable emphasis on closure, is further reinforced by the details of plot in *As You Like It.* In *A Midsummer Night's Dream,* the young lovers' flight to the woods is precipitated by Egeus's sternness and his insistence on invoking "the sharp Athenian law." Once in the woods, the lovers move through a dazzling series of complications. Their difficulties are at the center of our attention, but the quarrel of Oberon and Titania engages us as well, and Bottom's plight provides still another focus of concern. Still, release from these entanglements is conveniently in the hands of Oberon (through his agent, Puck); and the opposition of Egeus, made moot by Demetrius's conversion, is silenced altogether by Theseus: "Egeus, I will overbear your will" (4.1.179). Moreover, Egeus as a blocking character is ineffectual at best, a sort of lightweight heavy father; his frequent stage portrayal as a feckless fussbudget seems exactly right. Set over against later versions of the same type character—Polonius, say, or Brabantio—and even allowing for the differences dictated by their tragic contexts, he seems an attenuated figure.

The blocking figures in *As You Like It,* though, present formidable opposition. Both Oliver and Duke Frederick bring to the stage a sense of iron implacability. Oliver's contempt for his brother (and for his late father's will) is underscored and made even uglier by his gratuitous disdain for Adam. Dismissing Orlando with a false promise of compensation, he orders the old retainer, "Get you with him, you old dog" (1.1.81). Duke Frederick's dismissal of Rosalind, falling without warning and with no apparent cause, makes him an appropriate soulmate for Oliver, a likeness made even more apparent by his disregard of Celia's feelings. Arguing for mercy to Rosalind, Celia speaks the language of innocent childhood affection:

> If she be a traitor,
> Why, so am I. We still have slept together,
> Rose at an instant, learn'd, play'd, eat together,
> And wherso'er we went, like Juno's swans,
> Still we went coupled and inseparable.
> (1.3.72–76)

When her father reiterates his banishment of Rosalind, Celia seems nearly broken—"Pronounce that sentence then on me, my liege, / I cannot live out of her company" (1.3.85–86)—but the Duke's icy reply shows how little he regards his daughter's hurt: "You are a fool" (87). Evil as Duke Frederick and Oliver seem in their behaviors, that impression gains even greater force in light of the associations they bring to the play through their connection with archetypal patterns. Oliver's violent disregard for ties of blood and family loyalty associates him with Cain, and his plotting with the wrestler Charles taints him, like Claudius, with "the primal eldest curse." Duke Frederick, having banished his brother, takes on in relation to Rosalind the role of stepfather and thus carries into the play, along with the ugliness of his particular actions, all the cultural baggage that role entails.

Thus the blocking figures in *As You Like It* are more potent than is usually the case, more deeply evil, and the bases of their opposition to the play's romantic principals, Orlando and Rosalind, are independent of one another. The implications of this for Shakespeare's dramatic strategy are fundamental, for he is required to liberate the lovers from their separate antagonisms in order to bring them together, and he is required to bring Oliver and Duke Frederick through separate transformations that will leave them, at the play's close, posing no threat to the emergent new social order. On the level of plot requirements, then, *As You Like It* focuses our attention on closure with a complex intensity.

In yet another way, the plot requirements of *As You Like It* call special attention to its close. The ceremonies that bring Shakespeare's comedies to their end are ordinarily joyous affairs and, typically, assemble most of the cast on stage to mark the transformations that have occurred and the new relationships that are to be cemented. No other comedy, however, has so many couples to be united (four in all); and in no other comedy are these unions dependent, up to the very end, on the sort of revelation introduced by Rosalind. In *Twelfth Night*, Viola's disguise must be shed before she can claim her right function as Orsino's "fancy's queen"; but Olivia and Sebastian are already wed. "Another Hero" must be unveiled in *Much Ado about Nothing*, but the audience knows that Benedick and Beatrice have come to an agreement earlier in the play. While Rosalind in actual practice controls only two of the matches at the end of *As You Like It* (hers with Orlando, Silvius and Phebe's), our impression in the theatre is that she orchestrates the entire ceremony. Whatever the case may be, it is certain that the complicated maneuverings required to bring these eight celebrants before Hymen, both the "country copulatives" and their courtly counterparts, arouse our expectations and thus focus our attention on the resolution Shakespeare provides.

The matters discussed so far, though they have extraordinary qualities about them, are comfortably within the range of our experience of comedy and require no great stretch of the methods of critical analysis that are generally employed in such cases. They do, however, have the effect of emphasizing the importance of closure. Three other aspects of the play reinforce that emphasis while at the same time making greater demands on the critical ingenuity that would attempt to understand them fully. The first of these three—two events, actually, brought together because their function is similar and because they belong to the same realm of experience—is the conversion experiences of Oliver and Duke Frederick. The second is the masquelike appearance of Hymen. The third, recently become more problematic under the pressure of feminist readings of *As You Like It*, is Rosalind's performance in the play's epilogue.

The conversion of Oliver, in an episode heavily layered with emblematic significance, asks to be read allegorically. Not merely the snake and the lioness but the oak, "whose boughs were moss'd with age / And high top bald with dry antiquity," and even Oliver himself, described as "a wretched ragged man, o'ergrown with hair" (4.3.104–106), combine to create a sort of interpretive puzzle for readers or spectators of the play. Given the tendency to locate meaning at the point of closure, it is not surprising that this passage, prelude to the brothers' reconciliation and the redemption of Oliver, should be seen by some as central to the play's intellectual design.

Oliver's conversion comes at a point when he is helpless and under attack. Duke Frederick's, no less miraculous, comes just at the point when he has "address'd a mighty power . . . purposely to take / His brother here, and put him to the sword" (5.4.156–58). The redemption of Oliver qualifies him as suitor for Celia; that of Frederick turns him away "both from his enterprise and from the world" (162). Both episodes invest the play's close with special interest and seem to attribute to the close a more than ordinary share of critical value.

Hymen's entrance (5.4.107), unannounced and unexplained, presents an open critical issue. Agnes Latham provides the terms that we think of as in part defining the question: "It is left to the producer to decide whether the masque shall be plainly a charade got up by Rosalind, or whether it is pure magic, like the masque in *The Tempest*, in which the actors were 'all spirits.' "[1] This seems remarkable latitude, and the producer's (director's) decision is bound to have a major effect on the overall tone of a production. Coming when it does, the episode is certain to influence in a profound way our perception of the play's end and is thus one more reason for seeing closure as especially important to our efforts to come to critical terms with *As You Like It*.

Rosalind herself remarks on the oddity of her final business in the play: "It is not the fashion to see the lady the epilogue." Not only is it not the fashion, it is so contrary to the fashion as to make critical news. On its surface, Rosalind's performance here is merely a clever manipulation of some of the ironies involved in having a female role played by a boy actor who, playing a woman, must disguise himself as a boy. The ironies are, of course, further compounded when the actor, as Rosalind, makes unmistakable reference in the epilogue to his true sexual identity. Not surprisingly, this passage has been seized upon by feminist critics as a key to the play's meaning, even though (again, not surprisingly) their views of that meaning differ considerably.

Thus *As You Like It* contains a great many elements that reinforce the critical habit of attending to closure and of discovering in closure the play's central significances. The results of this have been threefold. As with all the comedies, *As You Like It* has been viewed in the context of the Barber-Frye approach and understood in large part teleologically, judged by the ways in which its structure is essentially the unfolding of its significance. Second, the unusual character of some of the materials associated with the end of *As You Like It* has led critics to isolate those features and make them central to their reading of the play. While these readings may also involve a concern with structure, they are primarily directed at the extraordinary feature in itself and may, therefore, have little to do with the comic design that the followers of Barber and Frye emphasize. The third consequence of focusing on closure, one remarked consistently in my earlier discussions of the phenomenon, is the loss of attention to the play's moment-by-moment development and a resultant sacrifice in understanding of its comedy as opposed to its comic form.

It seems unnecessary to review at any great length the arguments of critics who pursue the Barber-Frye line in discussing *As You Like It*. Invariably, such critics stress a connection between closure and meaning, locating the comedy's significance in the events that bring it to an end. Most of those who see the play in this way manage to bring the striking, even miraculous matters of its last scenes into the realm of rational discourse. Applying their various analyses to the play's whole design, they bring us to an understanding of its shape and purpose so "that reason wonder may diminish" (5.4.139). Only occasionally will the sudden and miraculous conversions render a critic inarticulate or incoherent, as Ruth Nevo seems when the close of *As You Like It* leads her to metaphoric excess: "wickedness has burst, like a boil, by some mysterious spontaneous combustion, leaving not a rack behind."[2] More typical is the language of Charles Frey, whose reading of the play as "Comedy of Reconciliation" sees it as a movement "from the seemingly incommensurate and relative to the all-liked and from like as quirky preference to like as shared pleasure."[3] For Frey, "the play, after all, does move in a direction"; in that movement, Shakespeare "drives us from fortune into nature, from relativities of rank and luck toward happy glimpses of teleological harmonies" (14, 27). Anthony B. Dawson, regarding *As You Like It* from a perspective that emphasizes Shakespeare's dramatic strategies—techniques such as "illusion, deceit, disguise, and manipulation" that "radically affect the relation of the audience to the play"—sees that at the comedy's close "we are returned to everyday experience with a richer sense of the theatrical and a more expansive view of reality."[4]

The appearance of Hymen as presiding deity at the point of the play's resolution invests *As You Like It* with a more than ordinary sense of solemnity. Whether we take his appearance as something truly miraculous, an earnest manifestation of Rosalind's knowledge of magic, or whether we take some more mundane explanation and see the representation of the god as merely that, a device contrived by the heroine, the event still stands for something beyond itself. That is, Hymen as supernatural phenomenon and Hymen as representation alike bring in their wake symbolic or emblematic significances. For G. K. Hunter, the episode suggests that Rosalind's control over the play world "seems to be supported by a force outside herself or a tendency in the world—call it the Life-force if you will; Hymen is as good a name as any, and Shakespeare does not seem too anxious to make definitions—which can emerge and take charge on their own account, when this is required."[5] Harold Toliver registers a similar sense of this power displayed in the play's closing ceremonies: "the inverted and unnatural relations of lovers and brothers, duke and subject, and the rudeness and incivility are overcome by the marriage rite and its implicitly multilayered social contract."[6] For R. Chris Hassel, the wholeness and reconciliation found by Hunter and Toliver in the masque are even more strikingly demonstrated in Rosalind's epilogue. By this device, "frankly admitting the stage's realistic limits and thus merging play world and audience world," Shakespeare "obviates the desire either to identify the two or to choose between them."[7] In this way, Rosalind's performance constitutes "an invitation to festive communion" (22) and thus brings us to the final end of Shakespeare's comic design.

One of the noteworthy features of the Barber-Frye line of criticism is its nearly endless adaptability. Earlier, in chapter 1 and elsewhere, I have pointed out how the most unfestive readings of individual plays will still isolate the play's closure as the locus of its meaning. Some of the critical methodologies in recent favor have either rendered such interpretations problematic or dispensed with them altogether.[8] Popular critical operations of recent years have certainly altered many once-familiar analytical procedures and overthrown others, but old critical habits—like habits of every sort—die hard. It is instructive to look from the perspective of this study at some recent efforts to come to terms with *As You Like It*. These efforts to understand the play are not isolated "readings," nor are they in the main concerned with the issues of structure and closure so central to Barber, Frye, and their followers. Still, a close look at these analyses suggests, first, that the reading as a procedure continues in new ways and in places where we might not expect to find it, and, second, that an emphasis on the conjunction of closure and meaning remains one of the commonest outcomes of such a procedure.

Peter Erickson's account of *As You Like It* provides a useful starting point, simply because he acknowledges directly his commitments to earlier critical views even while he puts forth a revisionist interpretation of the play's meaning. A student of C. L. Barber, Erickson affirms the basic terms of his mentor's approach to comedy. The issue of comic drama, for Erickson, is the meaning discoverable in its closing action. What is new about his reading is that he joins his training in familiar methods with a feminist ideology that allows him to overturn certain long-held assumptions about the meanings embodied in *As You Like It*.[9]

Admiration for Rosalind has been the key response to the play for generations of critics. From the effusiveness of Mrs. Jameson through the cynicism of Shaw and up to and including critics of far more rigid methodologies, she has been almost universally beloved:

> She is like a compound of essences, so volatile in their nature, and so exquisitely blended, that on any attempt to analyze them, they seem to escape us.

> In her nature throughout there is in rare union the most just balance of the powers of feeling and intelligence; the sensibility of Viola and the wit of Beatrice are blended in her.

> The popularity of Rosalind is due to three main causes. First, she only speaks blank verse for a few minutes. Second, she only wears a skirt for a few minutes (and the dismal effect of the change at the end to the wedding dress ought to convert the stupidest champion of petticoats to rational dress). Third, she makes love to the man instead of waiting for the man to make love to her—a piece of natural history which has kept Shakespeare's heroines alive, whilst generations of properly governessed young ladies, taught to say "No" three times at least, have miserably perished. . . . Who ever failed, or could fail, as Rosalind?

> In her conception Shakespeare is at last able to express at once engagement and detachment,the capacity to feel as well as to control emotion,

> the commingling in her temperament of feeling and judgment in perfect equilibrium. It is this which makes Rosalind the dramatist's climactic achievement in his search for a comic heroine who would express in word and act a particular comic vision.

> Rosalind is thus all a woman can be. Emotionally committed to femininity yet sexually experienced in both male and female attitudes, she remains witty and skeptical enough never to be trapped in an inexpedient role.[10]

One common basis of these encomiastic tributes lies in the belief that Rosalind, controlling and directing the main actions of the play, is a figure of commanding power. In what one might call a naive feminist perspective, Rosalind ranks above even such characters as Portia, Beatrice, and Viola; her combination of wit, imaginative energy, and good sense makes her seem the embodiment of Shakespeare's belief in the natural superiority of women. Erickson confronts this notion and displaces it not merely by attending to the character Rosalind but by looking as well at the emergence in the famous epilogue of the boy actor playing the heroine's role. Where earlier critics notice charm and wit, Erickson discovers grounds for understanding that "*As You Like It* is primarily a defensive action against female power rather than a celebration of it" (37). Instead of seeing the epilogue as Rosalind's (i.e., a woman's) ultimate witty triumph, he sees it as the reduction of the stage, in Rosalind's assertion of her boy identity, to an all-male preserve. Thus the structure of the play is patriarchal, and "the sense of the patriarchal ending in *As You Like It* is that male androgony is affirmed whereas female 'liberty' in the person of Rosalind is curtailed" (34–35).

Whatever designation we may use for Erickson's criticism, it is clearly not naive feminism. In its stress on a repressive patriarchy it provides a radical rereading of Rosalind and thus sets itself against the most widely held views of the play. Nevertheless, Erickson's reading lies comfortably within the circle of those approaches that emphasize closure, finding in the play's end not merely its conclusion but its theme and purpose as well. Richard Levin's recent strictures on feminist criticism are relevant in this context, for Levin sees—rightly, I think—that the pursuit of ideological theses may blind critics to fundamental structural and theatrical realities within individual plays.[11] This is especially the case with comedy, where ideology as teleological impulse may almost wholly dampen the elements of variety and play that bring the comedies to life on the stage.

One of the most influential recent essays on *As You Like It* is "'The Place of a Brother' in *As You Like It*: Social Process and Comic Form."[12] In that essay, Adrian Louis Montrose does a masterly job of applying the insights of anthropology, psychology, and social history to an effort to understand Shakespeare's comedy. While Montrose's work is not, in this case, quite a paradigm of the usual operations of new historicist methodology—we miss, for example, the telling and sometimes far-fetched anecdote that often serves as the surprising entryway into essays of this kind—it shares enough features of the genre to support our viewing it in the context of that critical movement.

Montrose's discussion is both wide-ranging and complex. In describing its major arguments, I mean neither to conceal their subtlety nor to quarrel with their premises. What I wish to show is simply this: for all its newness, both in what it has to say and in the marshaling of its evidence from such a rich variety of sources, the essay is tied in fundamental ways to procedures and assumptions we associate with Barber and Frye. For Montrose, *As You Like It* is *about* a whole complex of sociopolitical issues: sibling rivalry, the passage from adolescence to adulthood, primogeniture, son-father relationships, hierarchy. It is the business of the play to manage these issues, to incorporate them into its design, and to bring them to a resolution. "The form of *As You Like It*," Montrose writes, "becomes comic in the process of resolving the conflicts that are generated within it; events unfold and relationships are transformed in accordance with a precise comic teleology" (29). Finally, Montrose urges that the purposiveness of the comedy is tied to patriarchy and its requirements. While he does not wish to deny Rosalind's brilliance, neither does he wish to extend her any extraordinary social power: "If *As You Like It* is a vehicle for Rosalind's exuberance, it is also a structure for her containment" (52). In the world of the play, as in the world it reflects, "solutions to conflicts are worked out between brother and brother, father and son—among men" (52).

Given such an emphasis, it is not surprising to see that Orlando is the central focus of Montrose's reading. The identification between process and form in Montrose's title is nearly complete: "In *As You*

Like It the process of comedy accomplishes successful passage between ages in the life cycle and ranks in the social hierarchy. By the end of the play, Orlando has been brought from an impoverished and powerless adolescence to the threshold of manhood and marriage, wealth, and title" (30). The comedy, Montrose claims, "is both a theatrical *reflection* of social conflict and a theatrical *source* of social conciliation" (54). *Process, form, comic teleology, social conciliation*: all these terms direct our attention to the nexus of closure and meaning. As in so many similar cases, critical gains are offset in part by corresponding critical losses. What the comedy reflects and what it achieves obscure—in fact, displace—what it is and does.

Other recent discussions of *As You Like It* reveal something like the same pattern observed in the work of Erickson and Montrose. I think especially of the approach to the play followed by Marilyn Williamson in *The Patriarchy of Shakespeare's Comedies.* Although Williamson is explicitly uninterested in providing readings of the plays she discusses, she nevertheless finds in *As You Like It* the pattern familiar from Barber's discussion of the work: "Rosalind's disguise, her holiday humor, her claims to magic power, all relate her stay in the forest to festivals and rituals which give topsy-turvy power to women."[13] The difference, of course, is that her focus is almost exclusively on Rosalind. Still, this focus allows her to see the play's chief meaning to emerge at its close "when Rosalind doffs her disguise" and when, in the presence of her father, she "accents her shift from daughter to wife, both subordinate roles, as all atone together" (47).

At the close of his discussion of *As You Like It* in *The Heart's Forest,* David Young pauses to note that his praise of the play has focused chiefly on its stylistic features. He finds such a focus appropriate, however, "because *As You Like It* is, in fact, almost all style, accomplishing its ends through stratagems of language, brilliant verbal juxtapositions."[14] Like most such absolute assertions, in literary criticism as in life ("You always say that"), this one exaggerates its point for the sake of the immediate argument and thus requires some modification if it is to gain full support. Style alone, in Young's sense of the term, can hardly explain the stage popularity of *As You Like It.* The play is a perennial favorite in the theatre, and its popular esteem, while owing something to matters of style, seems founded chiefly on elements of character and plot. This may be a quibble; but if so, it is one that turns on fundamental questions about the nature of comedy in a play whose meanings have been canvassed extensively but whose comic energies as they unfold moment by moment on the stage have received far less attention.

What is the nature of the comedy in *As You Like It*? Harold Jenkins, in an influential essay, argued that the play "is conspicuously lacking in comedy's more robust and boisterous elements"; but the key to its difference from the other major comedies, he went on to say, "is in the defectiveness of its action . . . in its dearth not only of big theatrical scenes but of events linked together by the logical intricacies of cause and effect."[15] Although some critics have demurred from this judgment, a large majority have agreed with Jenkins, regarding *As You Like It* as a comedy whose effects depend very little on Shakespeare's design and management of plot.

The views of Young and Jenkins are alike, I believe, in a fundamental way. I don't mean simply that they emphasize similar features of the play: Jenkins, for example, finds "In *As You Like It* the art of comic juxtaposition at its subtlest" (33), while Young describes how the work invites its spectators and readers "to view the pastoral convention simultaneously from the inside, as in Lodge, and from the outside, as a frankly artificial and illusory construction" (70). I mean, rather, that both critics, caught up in an abstract intellectual analysis of the play, tend to ignore the possibility (the likelihood, I would say) of a more direct and immediate response to Shakespeare's comedy. To the average theatergoer, the plot elements of *As You Like It* are not mere devices to get the characters to the forest. They are of fundamental interest and remain so from beginning to end. Oliver's unfounded hatred of his brother—"my soul (yet I know not why) hates nothing more than he" (1.1.165–66)—is reinforced by the stern injunction of Duke Frederick: "bring him dead or living / Within this twelvemonth, or turn thou no more / To seek a living in our territory" (3.1.6–8). Orlando is thus, from the viewpoint of plot, never wholly out of danger until the end of act 4, after Oliver's conversion. Even at that point, the elder brother's villainy is intensified by one of those tricks Shakespeare uses from time to time to supplement the onstage action. Oliver's report to Rosalind and Celia earns him a barrage of questions:

> Cel. Are you his brother?
> Ros. Was't you he rescu'd?
> Cel. Was't you that did so oft contrive to
> kill him?
>
> (4.3.133–34)

"So oft" in Celia's query misstates the case, but like Emilia's comment on the handkerchief in *Othello*—"My wayward husband hath a hundred times / Woo'd me to steal it" (3.3.292–93)—it has the effect of darkening the evil to which it points.

Banishment is Rosalind's lot as it is Orlando's; and while no direct threat to her well-being dominates our concern for her situation, she does sustain the burden of the love plot once she and Celia establish themselves safely in Arden. For scholars and critics familiar with pastoral, knowledgeable about Lodge's *Rosalynde*, and at home with the conventions of romance and romantic comedy, plot as it relates to Rosalind is a matter of manipulating well-known counters, not the discovery of an astonishing solution. For less well trained readers or spectators of the play, her situation is a continuing source of pleasurable uncertainty, and her solutions to the difficulties that situation entails—from her enlisting as tutor to Orlando to her deft management of Phebe—have about them something of comic genius.

The same is true for the stylistic elements of the play. What Young finds so consistently engaging at the level of "verbal juxtaposition"—and Young here, like Jenkins, stands as a convenient representative of widely held critical attitudes—is likely to appear to members of a popular audience as a clash of attitudes defined chiefly in terms of character. No doubt a particular flash of verbal brilliance will occasionally sustain itself in the minds of the spectators I imagine here, but what critics see as Shakespeare's manipulation of stylistic and rhetorical effects they are more likely to see as the spontaneous expression of attitudes defined and articulated by the play's characters.

For these reasons, I tend to see the comedy of *As You Like It* as comedy of character. What that means in terms of the play's unfolding design I hope to define in the pages that follow. But before doing that, I want to suggest other dimensions of the play's comedy (both its sources and its mode of presentation by Shakespeare) that lend support to such an emphasis. The playwright's debt to Lodge's *Rosalynde* is one important source of the impression his comedy makes in *As You Like It.* One usual approach to the question of Shakepeare's handling of his source materials is to stress differences, to point out how he redefines questions of causation or subtly alters relationships to suit his own dramatic purposes. In *As You Like It* such shifts include his making the exiled duke and his usurper brothers, thus echoing the fraternal conflict between the younger men, and his not giving to Orlando a richer inheritance from his father than is bequeathed to either of his elder brothers.

Critics tend less frequently to dwell on the ways in which Shakespeare is guided by his source, not merely in shaping details of plot or in stressing particular themes but in the movement of events and their presentation. Lodge's fiction is more remarkable for its divisions than for its continuity. Passages of narration will suddenly come to an end, giving way to set pieces—monologues, dialogues, sonnets, poems for two voices—that illustrate the preceding narrative or advance it while reflecting its thematic concerns. The titles of some of these—"Saladynes meditation with himself," "Alindas oration to her father in defence of faire Rosalynde," "A pleasant Eglog betweene Montanus and Coridon," "Saladynes discourse to Rosader unknowen"—may give an idea of their function in *Rosalynde.*[16] Shakespeare, of course, employs no such obvious divisions; still, *As You Like It* at some level reflects Lodge's storytelling habits. Shakespeare's mode in this play is far more presentational than in any other of his major comedies. It is tempting to say that his chief device of presentation is the duologue rather than the dialogue, for again and again he sets before us two characters who provide exposition, argue opposed positions, or simply take up roles without any sense that their performances are generated by the necessity of moving the dramatic situation forward.

In this way, *As You Like It* manifests certain of the features of Lyly's comedy as defined some years ago by Michael R. Best.[17] It may even be that this static quality derives from a narrative impulse that manages, in this instance, to claim precedence over Shakespeare's usual manner of handling his comic material. Since the set piece is such a dominant device in *As You Like It,* it is no wonder that many critics find the play chiefly engaging at the level of style. Still, even the strongest partisans of the play find it hard to defend Touchstone's analysis of "a lie seven times remov'd" (5.4.68), or his pointless nonsense (it deserves the tautology) about the knight, the mustard, and the pancakes (1.2.63–80); and his praise of horns (3.3.48–63), for those of us old enough to recall it, seems no more amusing than the rote exchange beginning "Tough." "What's tough?" "Life." "What's life?" "A magazine." But Touchstone, whatever precedence in wit he may claim by virtue of his place as court fool, is neither the prime source of wit nor the cause of wit in others in *As You Like It*, and I think that "style" in the play is finally more a matter of attitude and a sense of self than it is a matter of language per se.

A final source of comedy in *As You Like It* grows out of what might be called its analytical disposition. A good many critics have spoken of this tendency in the play, and it seems appropriate to note that it is a tendency rooted deep in the pastoral tradition.[18] While the habit of analysis, pursued in one direction, may lead to praise or celebration (at times to affectionate exposure of limitations), it may on the other hand lead to criticism and rejection. This is only to say that the pastoral and the satiric modes are opposite sides of a single coin. As pastoral, the play is committed to analysis, the exploration of questions of value, and finally celebration. As satire, it is committed to ridicule and to the exposure of misjudgment and folly. Both modes are productive of comedy, and it is Shakespeare's particular skill in the play to balance them in a way that produces its distinctive humor. This is the quality that for many critics defines the special richness of *As You Like It*—a richness that seems, more than in any of the other comedies, deeply connected to our own habits of analysis, with their polar tendencies of celebration and rejection, blame and praise.

As You Like It, by general agreement, falls between *Much Ado about Nothing* and *Twelfth Night* in the chronology of Shakespeare's plays. It is no sign of mere bardolatry to say that the playwright's craft in structuring these three comedies illustrates his commitment to experimentation within the limitations imposed by his materials and to argue further that his theatrical genius appears strikingly in the methods he uses to open each play's action. *Much Ado about Nothing* begins with a long scene (328 lines) of news, gossip, homecoming, witty antagonism, male camaraderie, and romantic plotting. Conflict as a mainspring of comic action barely emerges here, for the scene closes with Don Pedro's assuring Claudio that he will both court Hero on his behalf and represent his case to her father, and his asserting, in a spirit of energetic good fellowship, "the conclusion is, she shall be thine" (1.1.327). The excited pace of all this has the effect of drawing us directly into the action. Shakespeare introduces us to all the characters who will matter to us over the course of the play, and he establishes a tone of realism that focuses our attention on characters plotting rather than on characters operating within, and controlled by, a plot.

Set against such a procedure, the opening of *Twelfth Night* seems highly artificial. The contrast between Illyria and Messina is more than striking. As Orsino's dukedom emerges, it does so in a series of brief scenes, each of which defines a significant dramatic question. Will Orsino win Olivia? How will Viola make her way in this world?[19] Can Sir Andrew succeed in *his* courtship of Olivia, or (more reasonably) can Sir Toby continue to delude his puppet and thus guarantee a continuing supply of cakes and ale for himself? Can Viola negotiate the difficulties imposed by her disguise as, loving Orsino, she must serve as his ambassador to Olivia? At some level, each of these questions becomes a question about the playwright, about his skill in manipulating characters and events. By the end of 1.5, the plot events have become dizzying, and we as spectators or readers are fully conscious of them well before Viola sets them before us in all their challenging complexity:

> How will this fadge? My master loves her dearly,
> And I (poor monster) fond as much on him;
> And she (mistaken) seems to dote on me.
> What will become of this?
>
> (2.2.33–36)

The force she calls on—"O time, thou must untangle this, not I"—is certainly, in the play's design, a benign providence or fate; but we know, and we feel this as the play unfolds, that another name for so kindly an agent is William Shakespeare.

The contrast I am describing here is between a play whose unfolding seems natural and spontaneous and whose characters seem to be discovered in the act of shaping their own destinies, and a play whose action consistently borders on the incredible. *Much Ado about Nothing* runs the risk of earning full credulity and thus sacrificing the comic perspective that allows us to dismiss Don John lightly and to accept Claudio's shallow repentance for the real thing. *Twelfth Night* seems consistently exposed to the danger that we might "condemn it as an improbable fiction" (3.4.127–28) and thus deny the power and humanity of its comic wonder.

The opening of *As You Like It* shares something with each of the plays that surround it. Like *Much Ado about Nothing,* it engages us at the level of plotting rather than plot. Orlando is determined to escape the oppression of his brother, while Oliver, acting on the hatred that drives him so inexplicably, searches for a means to rid himself of one who makes him "altogether mispris'd" (1.1.170–71). Like the earlier play, too, *As You Like It* introduces its central female characters (in 1.2) not under the pressure of a significant plot complication but in a moment of leisurely talk where the rather bald exposition is taken care of summarily only to give way to merriment, the devising of "sports," and chatty teasing about "falling in love" (1.2.25). At the same time, *As You Like It,* in common with *Twelfth Night,* makes us aware of the playwright's shaping hand. It does so through its use of familiar motifs of romance (fraternal opposition within the de Boys family and between the two dukes, Rosalind and Celia's adopted disguises) and through its transparently artificial exposition.

Yet *As You Like It* also illustrates in its opening scenes a quality that it can claim as its own, and one that distinguishes it from the plays that come immediately before and after. Provisionally, I would like to call this characteristic the performative dimension of *As You Like It.* By this term I mean to signify a stance that the characters take within the play, a position that locates them somewhere between the relatively realistic behavior of Beatrice and Benedick and the plot-driven confusion and helplessness of Viola. Orlando's introduction in 1.1 provides a clear example. His opening lines ("As I remember, Adam . . . ") describe both the source of his current low state and his resolve to rebel against his brother's ill treatment. They are nearly straightforward exposition, differing from a narrator's account only in the bias attributable to their being spoken by an interested party. When Adam announces the coming of Oliver, however, something rather surprising takes place. Orlando readies the stage for the action that follows: "Go apart, Adam," he orders, "and thou shalt hear how he will shake me up" (1.1.27–28). The force of "Go apart" as a command will depend, in the theatre, on a director's view of what makes the following lines most efective. Adam, in any event, must intervene (at 1.63) after Orlando has collared his brother—perhaps even thrown him to the ground. Before that he may be merely a silent spectator of the brothers' argument, or he may be both silent and concealed from Oliver's view. Whatever the case, Orlando's directive to "Go apart" has the effect of placing Adam in the role of audience and making the younger brother's reaction to his elder's hostility less an instance of spontaneous irritation than a performance. What Orlando intends Adam to witness is not how Oliver will "shake [him] up" but his aggressive and calculated reaction to that shaking up.

The encounter with Oliver, then, provides Shakespeare with further room for exposition, but it provides Orlando with a space in which to act out his aggressiveness and make a case for himself before a sympathetic audience. The self-conscious allusiveness of his speech in its reference to the prodigal son—"Shall I keep your hogs and eat husks with them? What prodigal portion have I spent, that I should come to such penury?" (1.1.36–39)—along with its bravado, carries a note of self-aggrandizement: "I am no villain. I am the youngest son of Sir Rowland de Boys" (56–57). Because the case Orlando makes runs up against Oliver's legitimate position as eldest brother, and especially because readers and spectators who know *King Lear* are bound to detect echoes of Edmund's plea to Nature in Orlando's setting "blood" in opposition to "the courtesty of nations," Shakespeare was well advised to give Oliver, at the close of the scene, the brief soliloquy in which he allows Orlando's great merits and admits to the groundlessness of his own hatred for his brother. But that is the outcome of the scene, its issue in terms of the play's overall plot. The center of the scene, its performative aspect, is Orlando, displaying for Adam in both the language of debate and the physical language of hand-to-hand combat the grounds for his claim that the spirit of his father "grows strong" in him (70).

Rosalind and Celia, like Orlando, begin their opening scene by carrying out the technical function of exposition. Again, the performance of that function is rather flat and mechanical, qualities that support Harold Jenkins's view that in the play's first act "Shakespeare's haste to get ahead makes him curiously perfunctory" (31). But the real business of this scene is performance, and both women turn gladly from talk of banishment to talk that serves chiefly as a means of exhibiting their vitality and wit, a means of display. This is not, however, a sure-fire performance opportunity. Unlike Orlando's opening display, which benefits from the use of Adam as onstage audience and enjoys as well the stimulus of exciting physical action, the dialogue of Rosalind and Celia has to carry itself. In some productions it is also asked to convey thematic import in a way that stultifies its charm, and Fortune and Nature as pastoral themes become burdens too heavy for the actresses to bear.[20] Nevertheless, it seems clear that the opportunity is there—for performers witty enough to seize it—to generate true comic energy through self-display.

No doubt the attitudes toward love, Fortune, and Nature help to define the characters and to elucidate familiar pastoral concerns. But they seem more important here as vehicles for performance. Thus Anne Barton's laconic note to Rosalind's spirited contradiction of her cousin seems wholly appropriate. Rosalind says, "Nay, now thou goest from Fortune's office to Nature's. Fortune reigns in gifts of the world, not in the lineaments of Nature" (39–42); and Barton provides the following gloss: "41. **gifts . . . world**: i.e. wealth, power, and the like, as contrasted with beauty and intelligence, the gifts of Nature. This distinction was an Elizabethan commonplace."[21] What is said thus seems far less important than how it is said. Rosalind and Celia, so intent on this game that even the bumptious Touchstone must wait his turn to speak while they bring their version of "Can You Top This" to a close, show through performative display their readiness for the games that follow in *As You Like It*.

Other players emerge as well: Touchstone, first at court and then, more memorably, in Arden, and—in the forest—Jaques, Duke Senior, Corin, Amiens, and others whose participation is limited but who reinforce the play's dominant performative mode and, through its employment, enrich its comedy. Before the play's action shifts to Arden, however, it completes the business of separation with

Frederick's banishment of Rosalind and Orlando's flight from his brother's murderous schemes. The threats facing hero and heroine are severe. John Russell Brown pointed out long ago, and it has become a commonplace to note, that such threats appear in all the comedies.[22] Here, Rosalind is to depart within ten days and to come no nearer to the court than twenty miles upon penalty of death. "If you outstay the time," declares the Duke, "upon mine honor, / And in the greatness of my word, you die" (1.3.88–89).[23] Adam's fearful report makes the dangers Orlando faces seem even more terrifying. Oliver, the old servant says,

> this night . . . means
> To burn the lodging where you use to lie,
> And you within it. If he fail of that,
> He will have other means to cut you off;
> I overheard him, and his practices.
> This is no place, this house is but a butchery.
> (2.3.22–27)

Nevertheless, the force of these threats dissolves almost immediately. In the design of 1.3, Duke Frederick's outburst is only a minor interruption between two sets of game playing. In the first, the lovesick Rosalind declares that her affections "take the part of a better wrastler than myself" (1.3.22–23) and turns the jesting of her cousin into a declaration of love. In the second, the women move from grief at Duke Frederick's sentence of banishment to an animated discussion of their strategy for survival in the forest:

> Cel. I'll put myself in poor and mean attire,
> And with a kind of umber smirch my face;
> The like do you. . . .
> Ros. Were it not better,
> Because that I am more than common tall,
> That I did suit me all points like a
> man? . . .
> Cel. What should I call thee when thou art a
> man? . . .
> Ros. But what will you [be] call'd?
> (1.3.111–13, 114–16, 123, 126)

In all this, we see Rosalind and Celia acting for one another, not merely settling a strategy but playing out, in gesture and posture, the tactics they mean to employ. This performative comedy shifts the tone of the scene, allowing an audience to share their view that they "go [. . . in] content / To liberty, and not to banishment" (137–38). His means are different, but in 2.3 Shakespeare brings Adam and Orlando to the same resolution. Adam's savings provide a convenient sort of insurance as Orlando determines to reject the self-seeking and self-destructive "fashion of these times" and in their place "light upon some settled low content" (2.3.59, 68).[24]

Touchstone, of all Shakespeare's fools, seems to me the most problematic. He is so not because his fooling is tinged with sadness sufficient, like Feste's, to disturb for some spectators and readers the comic balance of the play in which he appears. Nor is he problematic because, like Dogberry, his obtuseness defies all probability. Rather, Touchstone presents difficulties because he is at once too much a part of the play and too little a part of it. As an actor on stage he fully embodies the performative element of *As You Like It*: he is always "on." As a character in the play, his performative behavior often seems irrelevant both to the comedy's design and to the comic life around him.

David Young, who has high praise for Touchstone, nevertheless provides useful support for this view of the fool's deficiencies. Quoting Touchstone's response to Jaques—"As the ox hath his bow, sir, the horse his curb, and the falcon her bells, so man hath his desires; and as pigeons bill, so wedlock would be nibbling" (3.3.79–82)—he describes it as "one of those moments . . . when Touchstone seems to me to bear an uncanny resemblance to W.C. Fields" (53, n. 13). The passage just quoted, in its rhythm and in its theme of self-exculpation, does strike one as perfectly suited for a Fieldsian delivery. But once the connection is made, it is easy to see that Touchstone functions throughout *As You Like It* as a stand-up comedian, a figure never wholly integrated into the play's overall movement. At times, his rather localized performances are wonderfully effective; at others, as I have suggested earlier, they seem a needless effort.

But if Touchstone's efforts often fall short or seem superfluous, most of the play's performative actions do not. These performances frequently take the form of what Young calls "comic duets, some, like Jaques' encounter with Touchstone, reported, most others overheard not only by the audience but by one or more of the other characters" (61). The forest seems to provide a natural stage for such performances. No sooner do Rosalind and Celia enter Arden, accompanied by the lagging Touchstone, than they spy "a young man and an old in solemn talk" (2.4.20–21); but the conversation between Corin and Silvius quickly becomes one-sided as the younger man lectures the elder on what it means to love. Cataloguing the behaviors that define the lover, Silvius caps his account with a definitive performance gesture:

> Or if thou hast not broke from company
> Abruptly, as my passion now makes me,
> Thou hast not lov'd.
> O Phebe, Phebe, Phebe!
>
> (40–43)

As he races off stage shouting his loved one's name, his extravagant display surprises none of the onlookers, and it moves Touchstone and Rosalind to thoughts of their own loves—Rosalind finding her wound in seeing Silvius's wound displayed, Touchstone in his memories of Jane Smile. Only Celia, unburdened by a current love or thoughts of a former one, looks to the travelers' immediate needs: "one of you question yond man, / If he for gold will give us any food" (64–65).

If the newcomers find Arden a place hospitable to performance, they are only discovering what we as spectators or readers have already learned. The play's second act opens with Duke Senior's praise of "this our life, exempt from public haunt" (2.1.15), and the rhetorical questions that he uses to launch his celebration mark it as performance. Amiens more than agrees:

> I would not change it. Happy is your grace
> That can translate the stubbornness of fortune
> Into so quiet and so sweet a style.
>
> (18–20)

He finds the Duke's performance itself worthy of praise. The Duke's first speech is itself a performance; his second, suggesting a hunt and yet lamenting that their prey, "native burghers of this desert city, / Should in their own confines with forked heads / Have their round haunches gor'd" (23–25), gives an opening for Shakespeare's introduction of Jaques. That introduction, by the First Lord, is performative comedy of a complex kind. The first part of the report is pure description, and its particularity and strange emotional weight must make the First Lord's role especially attractive to the lesser members of a company who are likely to contend for it:

> To-day my Lord of Amiens and myself
> Did steal behind him as he lay along
> Under an oak, whose antique root peeps out
> Upon the brook that brawls along this wood,
> To the which place a poor sequest'red stag,
> That from the hunter's aim had ta'en a hurt,
> Did come to languish.
>
> (29–35)

But the second part of his account, a description of Jaques's effort to "moralize this spectacle" (44) is from the actor's point of view (and ours as well) even more attractive and decidedly more complex. The actor is still in the performative mode, but the opportunity to relate the experience is now enriched by the opportunity to mimic the behavior of Jaques. Examples of the moralist's "thousand similes" (45) give way finally—perhaps because his forest companions have rewarded the First Lord's performance richly with their laughter and their acknowledgment of the accuracy of his impersonation—to a summary:

> Thus most invectively he pierceth through
> The body of [the] country, city, court,
> Yea, and of this our life.
>
> (58–60)

Thus performance here has both immediate and long-range implications. In its local function, the First Lord's turn helps to define the comic tactic that will dominate the scenes in Arden. Beyond that, it works as comic preparation, bringing Jaques before us so that when he arrives *in propria persona* he is a known quantity, a comic figure who can ground his performance on an audience's expectations.[25] When Jaques does appear in 2.5 he shares the performance space with Amiens, and the two of them alternate banter and song before an audience of Duke Senior's men. In Amiens's careful regard for Jaques—"It will make you melancholy, Monsieur Jaques"; "My voice is ragged, I know I cannot please you"; "What you will, Monsieur Jaques" (2.5.10–11, 15–16, 20)—one hears a tone of light mockery; Amiens is being solicitous, but his remarks are gauged to let his onstage audience (and the audience in the theatre) know that he is having sport with Jaques. Jaques, for his part, justifies the mockery as he displays his well-advertised fondness for moralizing: "More, I prithee more. I can suck melancholy out of a song, as a weasel sucks eggs" (2.5.12–13).

The contrast between Amiens's song (both the first "stanzo" and the one sung with the other foresters) and the "verse to this note" offered by Jaques is the contrast between a romantic pastoralism and a cynically realistic view of the choice of pastoral life. Although Jaques claims that the Duke "is too disputable for my company" (35), his own fondness for debate—really, for contradiction—is revealed in his answer to Amiens's song. Thematic material is here for those who seek it, but the comic force of the scene emerges in the play of characters, the mocking of the melancholic Jaques, and the satirist's revenge as he employs his "Greek invocation, to call fools into a circle" (59–60).

The comic preparation for Jaques remains in force even beyond his first appearance, for Shakespeare leads us to anticipate comic fun when Jaques and the Duke come together. "I love to cope him in these sullen fits" (2.1.68), says the Duke; and Amiens tells Jaques that the Duke "hath been all this day to look you" (2.5.32–33). When their meeting occurs, however, Jaques takes the focus off his own character by telling the Duke of his meeting with "a fool i' th' forest" (2.7.12). His description of Touchstone, "deep contemplative" as he "moral[s] on the time" (2.7.31, 29), serves a variety of comic purposes. It reinforces our view of Touchstone and thus works to keep his character before us, especially if the actor playing Jaques accentuates some tic of speech or gesture peculiar to his fellow actor's portrayal of the clown. While this differs somewhat from comic preparation, since we have already met the character, it serves some of the same functions. Even as Jaques's account affords the pleasures of mimicry, we see that the mimic is himself lacking in perception; the behavior he mocks, as many writers have observed, is precisely the behavior others find so mockable in him. Finally, the key to this comic moment is its performative dimension. From Jaques's entrance before the Duke, he is on stage in a double sense. The Duke's greeting to him—"Why, how now, monsieur, what a life is this, / That your poor friends must woo your company?" (2.7.9–10)—is inclusive in its intention; its broad humor seems calculated to summon his companions and direct the attention of the theatre audience to view Jaques as performer.

This scene that closes the second act has two additional instances of performative action. The first, Jaques's "seven ages" speech, is so familiar that contemporary critics tend to avoid commenting on it; the second, Amiens's song ("Blow, blow thou winter wind," 174ff.), is ordinarily discussed only briefly, and then in terms of the play's thematic materials. Both instances, however, deserve notice. Jaques's speech, however laden with commonplaces, is a brilliant theatre piece. No actor charged with its delivery has ever wished it shorter, and even the most jaded theatergoer must have some curiosity about how *this* actor in *this* production is going to bring the speech to life. The means of doing so are, of course, there in the text: in the description of the schoolboy "creeping . . . / Unwillingly to school" and of "the lover, / Sighing like a furnace"; in the rhythm that marks the soldier, "jealous in honor, sudden, and quick in quarrel"; through the sounds of age as the diminished voice "pipes / And whistles in his sound," and on to very oblivion. The speech is a perennially fascinating performative moment in productions of the play.

Amiens's song is performance of another kind. As the Duke calls on him—"Give us some music, and, good cousin, sing"—he obliges with a song that serves a dual function. Thematically, "Blow, blow thou winter wind" underlines themes of loyalty and friendship central to the pastoral tradition and to *As You Like It* in particular. Theatrically, it works to establish a tone mimed in the fellowship Orlando and Adam enjoy at the Duke's banqueting table and sealed in the Duke's closing gesture of the scene: "Give me your hand, / And let me all your fortunes understand" (199–200). The second act's concluding scene is filled, then, with performative actions; Shakespeare's stage, like the world it reflects, is "a wide and universal theatre" (137).

After the opening scene of act 3, in which Duke Frederick turns on Oliver, there are no "woeful pageants" in the theatre of *As You Like It*. Performative occasions abound, nearly all of them capable of providing the most rewarding sorts of stage comedy. Orlando's solo entrance in 3.2 and his precipitous exit ten lines later—"Run, run, Orlando, carve on every tree / The fair, the chaste, and unexpressive she" (9–10)—is only the first of these.[26] They continue in 3.2 through the mutual interrogation of Corin and Touchstone, the marvelous readings and mocking of Orlando's verses, and the long interview (with Celia as onstage audience) between Rosalind as Ganymed and the "fancy-monger" who "haunts the forest [and] abuses our young plants with carving 'Rosalind' on their barks" (364, 359–61).

Subsequent scenes continue the pattern. Touchstone's address to Audrey (3.3.48–63) seems wasted on her, but its rhetorical flourishes—"But what though? Courage!" "Horns? even so," "Is the single man therefore bless'd?" (51, 56, 58)—make comic sense as performance, especially before Jaques as hidden observer. Rosalind's rebuke of Phebe generates comic delight for both her onstage audience (Corin and Celia) and a theatre audience more likely than her companions to pick up the note of wistful self-reference in "thank heaven, fasting, for a good man's love" (3.5.58). Even such a slight moment as Rosalind's advice to Jaques on his departure takes on a richer and more complex comic tone when understood as a performative moment. "Farewell, Monsieur Traveller," she says,

> look you lisp and wear strange suits; disable all the benefits of your own country; be out of love with your nativity, and almost chide God for making you that countenance you are; or I will scarce think you have swum in a gundello.
>
> (4.1.33–38)

Considered at their surface level, these remarks offer a wonderfully comic instance of the satirist satirized, appropriate words of bon voyage to a Sir Politic Would-be. As performance, they give us Rosalind paving the way for her turn as Ganymed-as-Rosalind instructing her admirer in the ways of courtship: "Why, how now, Orlando, where have you been all this while? You a lover!" (38–40). Again, Celia as onstage audience helps to underscore the comic effect of Rosalind's performance; she is our surrogate and the leader of our appreciative chorus.

As Shakespeare brings *As You Like It* toward its conclusion, he continues to work in the performative mode. Rosalind's revelation to Silvius of Phebe's duplicity, conveyed in her reading of the country girl's poem, and Touchstone's mocking of William in 5.1 as he shows off for Audrey and for the theatre audience—"it is meat and drink to me to see a clown. By my troth, we that have good wits have much to answer for; we shall be flouting; we cannot hold" (10–12)—are two additional instances. Touchstone and Jaques in the set piece on quarreling and the seventh cause have one final comic duet, but the wit here (5.4.35–103) is flaccid at best and gives way to the play's greatest performance of all.

That performance is, of course, Rosalind's management of the multiple love alliances. Beginning with the "still music" that announces her entrance with Celia, accompanied by Hymen, she is the mistress of the play's close. The news of Duke Frederick's conversion and Jaques's decision to seek him out are necessary but minor details; they claim little stage time and even less of our attention. Our attention—fixed, as it has been throughout the play, on performative action—here focuses once again on the play's chief performer. The conjuration that has worked its magic over five acts is now made explicit; and acquiescing in the power of the actress—magic indeed—we bid her farewell.

five

Speaking Masterly

Comic Tone and Comic Preparation in Twelfth Night

mong the comedies, none has had more attention focused on its close than *Twelfth Night*. In part this can be explained with reference to the character of Malvolio, who stubbornly insists on his importance even to those critics who find no room for his antifestival spirit in the joyous world of Illyria. Dissatisfaction with the play's close on this score is not at all a recent phenomenon; John Russell Brown speaks of it in his 1955 survey of interpretation as arising from criticism based on the study of character.[1] But the more general reason for closure's status as a critical issue in understanding *Twelfth Night* lies in the play's position in the canon, where it is seen as bringing to an end the line of romantic comedy even as it bears the seeds of the darker plays to come. To see this is to find two related sources for emphasizing closure in *Twelfth Night*: genre criticism, the major development in study of the comedies over the last thirty years, and biographical criticism, often mocked since its formulation by Dowden but surprisingly capable of reappearing in unlikely places.

Without rejecting the clear achievements of recent critics, and without denying the relevance of genre criticism and studies of Shakespeare's development as a comic writer, it should still be possible to suggest an approach to *Twelfth Night* that takes pressure off its ending and judges it in terms of its overall function as dramatic comedy. What emerges will not be unfamiliar, but familiar things may, viewed from a different angle, seem new. The notion of plot provides a useful starting point. It is perhaps the most often employed element of analysis for fictions of all kinds; it permits (or requires) the invocation of Aristotle; and it places helpful emphasis on structure—beginning, middle, end.

What, then, can be said of plot in *Twelfth Night*? The short answer is "not much." Not much, that is, if plot is thought of as the soul of the comedy. Certainly one can chart a plot in the conventional way, with the impetus and shifts of direction reflected in the graph. But Shakespeare in *Twelfth Night* seems far less interested in plot than in plotting. His attention seems directed to short-term effects rather than to the solution of a comprehensive dramatic question. Moreover, it is the emphasis on plotting that allies him with the other great comic dramatists, with Jonson and Molière, for example, or in our own time with a master of comedy such as Tom Stoppard. Alexander Leggatt, noting the recurrence of comparisons between *Twelfth Night* and the comedies of Ben Jonson, speculates that any basis they have "may be in the sense of sharply distinguished individuals adrift in a fragmented world, each with his own obsession."[2] But a more fundamental similarity can be found in the preference of Jonson and Shakespeare, as comic writers, for short-term effects over comprehensive design, for plotting rather than plot.

The Alchemist, praised by Coleridge for its plot, affords an example of the distinction and its practical significance. The overarching plot, worked out within the strictest demands of the unities, is undeniably masterful. But a critic intent on discovering the sources of pleasure in Jonson's play would not find them in plot considered as overall design. Instead, such a critic would locate Jonson's primary achievement in his plotting, comic preparation that leads to ends predictable to an audience or reader but hidden from at least some of the play's characters.[3] Even such a minor matter as Mammon's entrance in 2.1 affords an instructive example, for its effect is to a very great extent dependent on Subtle's description of him in the preceding scene.

> Methinks I see him, entering ordinaries,
> Dispensing for the pox and plaguy houses,

> Reaching his dose; walking Moorfields for lepers;
> And off'ring citizens' wives pomander-bracelets,
> As his preservative, made of the elixir;
> Searching the spittle, to make old bawds young;
> And the highways for beggars, to make rich:
> I see no end of his labours. He will make
> Nature asham'd of her long sleep: when art,
> Who's but a step-dame, shall do more than she,
> In her best love to mankind, ever could.
> If his dream last, he'll turn the age to gold.[4]

Having enjoyed this preview of the character, we are primed for Mammon's imaginative and linguistic excesses as he enters with Surly: "Come on, sir. Now, you set your foot on shore / In *novo orbe*" (2.1.1–2).

But Jonson's triumph in this sort of comic preparation appears in Subtle's precisely timed "discovery" of Mammon after the horrified knight has loosed the tide of Doll's religious babbling. Subtle, having called from off stage, enters to witness the scrambling exits of Doll and Face. Mammon, alone with the reverend doctor, must bear his rebuke:

> *Mam.* Where shall I hide me?
>
> *Sub.* How! What sight is here!
>
> Close deeds of darkness, and that shun the light!
>
> Bring him again. Who is he? What, my son!
>
> O, I have liv'd too long.
>
> *Mam.* Nay, good, dear father,
>
> There was no unchaste purpose.
>
> *Sub.* Not? And flee me,
>
> When I come in?
>
> *Mam.* That was my error.
>
> *Sub.* Error?
>
> (4.5.33–39)

The energetic comedy of this scene, launched on the flood of Doll's raving, continues through a ludicrous parody of discovery in Eden, with Subtle as an implacable God and Mammon as a guilty Adam abandoned by his Eve. F. H. Mares, in his notes to the play, connects this episode (from its very beginning at the start of the fourth act) to the main plot, showing its place in relation to complication, crisis, and catastrophe.[5] As plotting, though, this nearly self-contained episode has an impulse and an outcome of its own. It is a measure of the play's energy that it presses forward from this moment with hardly a pause, propelled toward further confusion and discovery by the "*great crack and noise within*" (4.5.55) of the exploding apparatus.

Almost any of Jonson's plays could supply similar incidents. What *Twelfth Night* shares with Jonsonian comedy is an abundance of such comic events subsumed to the requirements of the play's major action but generating an energy that makes them almost independent episodes. Two instances of plotting on this level stand out. The first is, like Jonson's comic preparation for Mammon, a matter of introducing a character, in this case Olivia. But, as with most comparisons of Jonson and Shakespeare, the differences are instructive. Subtle's speech has a vivid particularity about it. He captures Mammon's habits of imagination, joining a view of alchemy as art beyond nature with the action of "searching the spittle, to make old bawds young" (1.4.23). Further still, Jonson's construction of the speech encourages the actor playing Subtle to treat the audience to a physical parody of the knight's figure and gestures before Mammon himself appears: "Methinks I see him."[6] Finally, the payoff in *The Alchemist* is immediate. After Subtle has given the audience a lesson on how to read Mammon, the knight himself appears, palpable and transparent.

Shakespeare's introduction of Olivia develops differently, and it does so in a way that reinforces the play's connection with the Feast of Epiphany; Sebastian is not alone in making a miraculous appearance in *Twelfth Night*. In the play's opening scene we learn of Olivia through Orsino, who gives first an unprompted view of her magical powers—"O, when mine eyes did see Olivia first, / . . . . / That instant was I turn'd into a hart"—and then an interpretation of Valentine's report, in which Orsino chooses not to see rejection of his suit but "a heart of . . . fine frame" (1.1.18, 20, 32).[7] The next three scenes of the play continue this line of plotting. Shakespeare never lets us forget Olivia's importance, and through the use of a marvelous dramatic retard he increases our eagerness to see her and the demands on the actress playing the role. She must meet the high expectations the playwright has set for her in scenes 1 through 4. In this respect, Shakespeare exploits the technique of delayed gratification, with the attendant risk of disappointing his audience, while Jonson, in the case of Mammon at least, is so eager to please that he unwraps his comic gift immediately.

Twelfth Night's fifth scene is the culmination of this plotting line considered as a discrete episode. Shakespeare unveils Olivia at last.[8] But even here the retard continues, for the scene begins with Feste and Maria, who warns the clown, as she had earlier warned Sir Toby, of her lady's displeasure. Olivia's initial verbal jousting with Feste performs two functions: it helps to separate her from the earnest solicitude of Malvolio, and it prepares her for the whimsical act of admitting the messenger, that figure described by Malvolio as "between boy and man," one who is "very well-favor'd," "speaks shrewishly," and looks as if "his mother's milk were scarce out of him" (1.5.155–62). Defeated in her contest with Feste, she chooses to continue the sport with a competitor who promises to be less skillful. What follows, of course, is one of the great comic confrontations in all of Elizabethan drama, and for a brief while I want to reserve comment on its detailed workings. As comic preparation, the whole of act 1, up through 5.26, works magnificently to establish a context for Olivia's appearance. When she does at last enter, she ought to be both as wonderful as Orsino suggests and more real than the creature of his delicate imaginings. She does not disappoint us. At once removed from the world and in it, she jokes with Feste and pronounces her authoritative judgment on Malvolio: "You are sick of self-love." Then she turns, or Shakespeare turns her, to enact yet another miraculous appearance, this time to Orsino's clamorous messenger.

The care Shakespeare lavishes on plotting of this sort appears in another episode in *Twelfth Night*, one quite different from the introduction of Olivia. This is the duel scene between Viola and Andrew, stage-managed by Sir Toby and Fabian. Again, the knitting of this incident to the main plot is brilliantly successful. Yet a spectator might be excused for discovering in the episode as a whole a sort of independent existence, a reason for being that extends no further than the creation of expectations in order to fulfill them in a moment of triumphant comic realization. Since Viola figures so prominently in most accounts of the play, it may be possible to sketch the plotting of the duel scene with primary emphasis on Sir Andrew, who has received less attention. Nevertheless, it should be clear that the duel scene achieves a doubling of the sort of effect seen in Jonson's introduction of Mammon. Here two characters are marshaled through a number of preliminary stages, then brought together in a pyrotechnic comic moment which is, strangely, at the same time a dud.

Sir Andrew's shortcomings as a wooer and linguist are so prominently set out in his first appearance (1.3) that Maria's comment on his reputation as a fighter is often overlooked. Andrew, she says, is "a great quarreller; and but that he hath the gift of a coward to allay the gust he hath in quarrelling, 'tis thought among the prudent he would quickly have the gift of a grave" (1.3.30–33). This is the first stage in Shakespeare's preparation for the duel. Even as the opening dialogue of scene 3 has as its immediate focus Andrew's first entrance, so it contains another purpose that will be slower in its development. "Is that the meaning of 'accost'?" "What is 'pourquoi'? Do or not do?" Sir Andrew's "three or four languages" fail him under the pressure of Maria's presence. Similarly, his gallantry dwindles into abashed incompetence under the dual demands of Maria's forthright challenge—"bring your hand to the butt'ry bar"—and the urging of Sir Toby. His bravery, however, will be put to a test only later, though with similar results.

Shakespeare advances this comic preparation next in the aftermath of Malvolio's interruption of the midnight revels (2.3). He does so, however, in an indirect way. Sir Andrew, casting about as usual in an effort to gain approval (often his method is simply to repeat the words of others), imagines a way to get back at the killjoy steward: " 'Twere as good a deed as to drink when a man's a-hungry, to challenge him the field, and then to break promise with him, and make a fool of him" (2.3.126–28). Sir Toby, quick to scent good fun, offers his full support: "Do't knight. I'll write thee a challenge, or I'll deliver thy indignation to him by word of mouth" (129–30). Maria, of course, has a better idea for Malvolio; and we can be grateful that Sir Andrew's inane plan does not occupy the dramatic space filled by the letter scene. But Shakespeare wastes neither Sir Andrew's empty gesture nor Sir Toby's offer of support: both function as preparation for the collision that will take place later in the play between Sir Andrew and the terrified Viola.

In 3.2 Sir Andrew petulantly announces that he is leaving, hurt by the sight of Olivia's favors to "the count's serving-man." Fabian then comes to the aid of Sir Toby, who is unwilling to lose his purse, and argues that Olivia's attention to Cesario was a pretense displayed for Sir Andrew's benefit. The countess's act was calculated, Fabian tells the disappointed suitor, "only to exasperate you, to awake your dormouse valor" (19–20). Andrew, he claims, has lost an opportunity: "You should then have accosted her, and with some excellent jests, fire-new from the mint, you should have bang'd the youth into dumbness" (21–23). Thus when Fabian offers Sir Andrew two ways to redeem Olivia's good opinion, valor or policy, Shakespeare has prepared us well for the knight's response: "And't be any way, it must be with valor, for policy I hate. I had as lief be a Brownist as a politician" (30–32). With this, Andrew is dismissed to write his challenge—"write it in a martial hand," says Sir Toby, "be curst and brief"—while he and Fabian turn our expectations up a notch higher as Shakespeare continues the plotting of the duel scene. Sir Toby knows what to expect: "I think oxen and wainropes cannot hail them together"; and yet the prospective combatants are well matched. "For Andrew," Sir Toby declares, "if he were opened and you find so much blood in his liver as will clog the foot of a flea, I'll eat the rest of th'anatomy"; and Fabian, speaking truer than he knows, observes that "his opposite, the youth, bears in his visage no great presage of cruelty" (42–43, 60–65).

While Andrew is thus by indirect and crooked ways led to the point of writing his challenge, Viola has been picking her way through the snares laid by her own disguise. With Orsino, she only narrowly refrains from self-discovery; with Olivia, she is torn between rivalry and loyalty to her master; with both, she gains a measure of relief by telling the truth riddlingly. Now, for the first time, she confronts a situation for which she has not prepared. Toby earlier had determined to convey Sir Andrew's challenge and "stir on the youth to an answer" (3.2.58–59). Now, having found the letter a perfect mirror of its author's ineffectuality, Toby decides to take the matter into his own hands—to challenge Cesario, persuade him of Andrew's fierceness, and "so fright them both that they will kill one another by the look" (3.4.195–96). The plan succeeds beyond Toby's fondest hopes. On the one side, Andrew offers to buy his way to safety ("Let him let the matter slip, and I'll give him my horse, grey Capilet"); on the other, Viola shrinks into an endearingly helpless aside ("A little thing would make me tell them how much I lack of a man" [3.4.285–87, 302–303]).

Then, as the reluctant duelists move toward one another and draw, the scene both fizzles and explodes. Antonio's entrance issues in the series of manifestations that will define the play's close and its final atmosphere of revelations, recognitions, and miracle. That is the explosion. Meanwhile, safely apart from the main action on stage, Viola and Andrew come together in mutual gratitude. Viola is all timid politeness—"Pray, sir, put your sword up, if you please"—while Sir Andrew, "as good as [his] word," pays a debt that, so far as Viola knows, he never promised—"He will bear you easily and reins well" (3.4.321, 323–34). What follows in the train of this great comic moment is the unfolding of layer upon layer of misapprehension and masking. But that unfolding should not obscure the immediate pleasure of the duel episode. Artfully designed, that episode furnishes an abundance of rewards both in the theatre and in the study. It takes its place in the total plot of the play, but its value is far greater than that of a link in the chain of plot or one piece (even a large piece) in a puzzle. In this respect, *Twelfth Night* is a less linear construction than most critics would have us believe. Its episodes have their own logic; they are not elements shaped wholly to serve the play's purposes as those are finally revealed at the point of closure.

In fact, *Twelfth Night* is of all Shakespeare's comedies least dependent on plot in the ordinary sense of that word. It finesses the whole idea of plot by appealing to another order of things. That order takes its most striking form (to seize an easy pun) in the appearances of Antonio and, later, Sebastian, where it provides experiences that are epiphanic in their nature. Its more pervasive and subtle form lies in an extraordinary reliance on atmosphere and tone. When Viola, in her role as Cesario, finally gains an audience with Olivia, Shakespeare's preparation has been so skillful that he has a variety of comic options available to him. The easiest of these—exploiting the physical or sartorial discomforts of disguise—he declines: at least so far as the text indicates; an actor might be free to improvise. But he ignores little else, from Viola's impatience as a loyal messenger and her jealousy of a beautiful rival to Olivia's mocking repartee and her sudden recognition of an access of love. This episode possesses such tonal variety that no criticism can do justice to it; and any single stage version, though it might capture some elements of that variety, would sacrifice others in being forced to make choices.

This much, though, should be clear. At the beginning of the encounter, the women are in different situations. Viola, who in 1.2 was the pattern of self-assurance and decisiveness, now exhibits those characteristics only in her assumed role. At Orsino's court, she is caught by her disguise, used as an emissary to woo on behalf of one she desires to wed. Olivia, secure as mistress of her house, claims strength from both her social position and her adopted role as mourning sister. By the scene's end, Olivia has caught the plague and Viola has discovered the beauty and wit of her rival. They have been reduced to a shared condition of hopeless yearning, a condition whose severity is revealed in each case in a moment of role playing. For Viola, this moment comes when Olivia asks her what she would do were she in Orsino's situation. In her reply,

> Make me a willow cabin at your gate,
> And call upon my soul within the house;
> Write loyal cantons of contemned love,
> And sing them loud even in the dead of night;
> Hallow your name to the reverberate hills,
> And make the babbling gossip of the air
> Cry out "Olivia!" O, you should not rest
> Between the elements of air and earth
> But you should pity me!
>
> (1.5.268–76)

Viola gains the opportunity to voice her own love as she enacts Orsino's, and many actresses in recent years have cried out " 'Or—Olivia' " to stress how far this displacement has overwhelmed the character's sense of her place and role. Olivia's role playing is not a moment of rapt forgetfulness but a precise recollection. To her own remembered question, she summons up Viola's reply: " 'Above my fortunes, yet my state is well: I am a gentleman!' "; and then she breathes out her response: "I'll be sworn thou art" (1.5.290–91).

The end of this encounter, completed for Viola by Malvolio's delivery of the ring, places the women in opposite but emotionally identical situations. Olivia loves a disguised female who cannot accept her overtures; Viola loves a male who believes her to be a boy. They declare a shared powerlessness in calling upon forces greater than those at their disposal, Olivia by an invocation—"Fate, show thy force; ourselves we do not owe"—Viola, more humbly, in an admission of weakness:

> O time, thou must untangle this, not I,
> It is too hard a knot for me t'untie.
> (1.5.310, 2.2.40–41)

The effect of this movement through 1.5 is to bring the two women, whose initial situation is so dissimilar, into a shared condition. They have both "caught the plague," and they are both constrained from taking steps to cure their lovesickness, Viola because she is now a prisoner of her disguise, Olivia by a complex of reasons, including the well-motivated elusiveness of the object of her love. Our attention, however, is focused not on what will happen to these characters, not on how Fate and Time will contrive to effect a solution to their problems, but simply on the facts of the problems themselves. Because Shakespeare achieves his effects through the deft manipulation of tone, the urgency of Viola and Olivia is only a small part of the spectator's or reader's experience. Instead, our focus is on the comic achievement; and our pleasure, a pleasure akin to satisfaction, comes from perceiving how Shakespeare has brought these two young women to the same pass, bound to wait in hope for the beneficial operation of forces that we know to be guaranteed by the laws of comedy itself.

Shakespeare's manipulation of tone, then, creates local and particular effects that gain for individual scenes and episodes their own importance. They are not merely way stations on the route to the play's end but ends in themselves which fulfill dramatic expectation, excite comic pleasure, and even provide vivid pre-enactments of closure that will make the play's actual ending seem less a surprising or problematic answer than a restatement of relationships and a reordering of matters that have already won our assent. No episode in the whole body of Shakespearean comedy registers these achievements so fully as *Twelfth Night* 2.4. Considered as an element in the play's plot, this scene appears nearly inconsequential. Orsino, attended by Viola, Curio, and others, calls for a song. Feste is summoned, performs the song, and—after some banter—departs. At Orsino's command, "all the rest give place" (79), and he is left alone with Viola, whom he directs to return to Olivia and once more plead his case. Then, after a brief dialogue that recapitulates matters familiar from the play's first scene, Viola recounts the history of her father's daughter, who "never told her love," but breaks off her account rather than respond to Orsino's desire to learn the story's closure: "But died thy sister of her love, my boy?" (110, 119).

Such a summary is not unfair if the scene is judged, at the surface level, in terms of its place in a movement toward closure. Going just beneath that surface, one might add that it has other effects. It extends the characterization of Orsino, helps to define Feste's prominence and freedom in the two households (Orsino's and Olivia's), increases the emotional pressure on Viola, and furthers dramatic tension by preparing for another encounter between Viola and an Olivia who, the messenger now realizes, has been "charmed" by her "outside" (2.2.18). But the scene has still greater importance. Its shape and mood controlled and directed by music and the art of storytelling, 2.4 does far more than recapitulate what we know of Orsino and advance the plot. On a technical level, it suggests a second realm of time, making the "three months" of the play's close more credible; it defines, in a telling way, the atmosphere of the Duke's court; and it reveals how far Viola has succumbed to that atmosphere.

The last of these effects is most important here. When Orsino calls for "the tune the while," the music provides a counterpoint to his sentimental address to Viola:

> Come hither, boy; if ever thou shalt love,
> In the sweet pangs of it remember me.
> (14–16)

Viola, under the joint spell of the music and Orsino's language, finds herself defenseless. If the tune moves Orsino to emotionally indulgent hints of mortality ("remember me"), the irony of his injunction only reinforces the oxymoronic "sweet pangs" she experiences even as he speaks. When Orsino, asking for confirmation of his own view, not independent judgment, asks, "How dost thou like this tune?" Viola speaks her own mind (or her own heart): "It gives a very echo to the seat / Where Love is thron'd" (20–22). The love between them, which only Viola can speak of, and then only in terms closed to Orsino's understanding, he nevertheless emphasizes in an unconscious pun: "Thou dost speak masterly" (22).

The union thus pointed to, which goes beyond shared feelings to posit a fundamental likeness and identity, Shakespeare strengthens as the scene moves to a close. Viola's story beginning "My father had a daughter loved a man" illustrates, from a point of view emphasizing the heroine's consistency—her independence, wit, inventiveness—a willingness to approach the danger of shedding her disguise. Such a reading purchases a consistent Viola, however, at the cost of a problematic ending. Viewed primarily in the context of the scene in which it appears, her story has another significance. Like Orsino's, Viola's love is shut within her, frustrated of expression. Like him, she turns to art for release. With no musicians at her command, Viola relies on storytelling, employing even the primitive form of the riddle. In her account, she does "speak masterfully," achieving an emotional intensity that she cannot control and regaining command of herself only with a transparent bravado like Rosalind's "counterfeit" after her fainting in *As You Like It* (4.3.166–82): "and yet I know not. / Sir, shall I to this lady?" (121–22).

In this early scene, then, Shakespeare has his characters pre-enact a closeness that is promised but deferred in the actual closure of the play. There, Orsino tells Viola, "you shall from this time be / Your master's mistress" (5.1.325–26); and yet he calls her Cesario until the end, though with the promise that "when in other habits you are seen" she will take up her true identity as "Orsino's mistress, and his fancy's queen" (5.1.387–88). Critics who find difficulty with the close of the play, especially those who find in it hints of darkness, fasten on this apparent incompleteness. Yet the fulfillment they miss is one of the pleasures *Twelfth Night* affords; it is not to be found at the close of the play, however, but in this scene, where Viola and Orsino come together in a wholly credible and persuasive way.[9] The tonal sureness of this scene is a major source of both its dramatic power and its clarity. It demonstrates early in the play the rightness of the design that finally brings Orsino and Viola together. Theirs may not be a marriage made in heaven, but it is made secure by this episode in Orsino's court. Thus Shakespeare's management of tone in 2.4 of *Twelfth Night* takes interpretive pressure off the play's ending, whose key union has been anticipated and even displayed for the audience's approval. The marriage of Viola and Orsino should not be viewed exclusively as either a festive triumph or a disenchanted comment on the failure of life to achieve the easy victories of comic convention. Its rightness is the rightness of comic drama, an order to which Shakespeare has gained our assent early in the play.

Other matters occur or are anticipated early in *Twelfth Night*, and this prematurity of events affords one last indication that Shakespeare asks less of his comic endings than his critics seem driven to ask. Chief among these is the audience's knowledge (from 2.1) that Sebastian is still alive, and the suggestion, and more than suggestion, to Viola (in 3.4) that her brother has not drowned after all. To a thoroughgoing believer in the strength of dramatic conventions, early disclosure of Sebastian's safety is hardly an issue. Viola herself, in her opening dialogue with the captain, provides hope if not assurance. To her wishful speculation "Perchance he is not drown'd," the captain offers no great comfort: "It is perchance that you yourself were saved" (1.2.5–6). But Viola continues to imagine a fortunate outcome: "so perchance may he be" (7). And of course one may enroll as a follower of E. E. Stoll and simply assert that in comedy shipwreck implies salvation, not death by water.

But the point, surely, is that in *Twelfth Night* Shakespeare takes all the burden off the question of whether and places it entirely on the question of how. Two aspects of his management of Sebastian's return suggest this emphasis. The first is the playwright's use of Antonio; the second, a pre-enactment of union for Olivia and Sebastian that repeats in another key that of Orsino and Viola in 2.4. In recent criticism, Sebastian's rescuer and benefactor has been made to seem a mere reprise of Antonio in *The Merchant of Venice*, and his justified pain has been regarded as springing from a frustrated homoerotic attachment. Such a reading lends an even greater darkness to the "problematic" interpretations of *Twelfth Night*. In terms of the play's comic needs, Antonio serves another role, one more concerned with the work's construction than with putative meanings. His entrance, rescue of Viola, and subsequent arrest bring the duel to a close and provide opportunity for revelations about Sebastian that excite Viola to hope her brother is alive. Since Viola's cowardice is now apparent to all, Sir Andrew's "dormouse valor" emerges again in his resolve to "after him again and beat him" (3.4.391).

Shakespeare might have brought Sebastian in at this point instead of Antonio, whose place in the play's final scene presents some difficulty because his function is so minimal. But Sebastian has to be saved for more important matters, first the great comic moment when Sir Andrew, mistakenly emboldened, strikes him and earns three for one—"Why, there's for thee, and there, and there!" (4.1.26), then his rescue by Olivia, who dismisses Toby ("Rudesby, be gone!") and takes Cesario's double under her rule. When Sebastian next appears he is in a golden dream, enrapt in wonder; and Olivia's entrance line—"Blame not this haste of mine"—achieves a high mark for the comic use of litotes, accompanied as the lady is by a priest and intent on securing "the full assurance" of Sebastian's faith (4.3.22, 26). Before the final act begins, then, Shakespeare joins Olivia and Sebastian just as he had earlier joined Viola and Orsino in a pre-enactment of their eventual union. In the latter case, the method involved a subtle use of tone reinforced by music; here he employs unrestrained farce and a full measure of physical action and fooling.[10] The upshot of all this means that with his final act Shakespeare can attend to other matters: to the resolution of the Malvolio line of action, and to the delight to be had in allowing the characters' understanding of matters to grow equal to the audience's knowledge.

That these are Shakespeare's main concerns can be seen in his handling of the skirmish that gives Sir Andrew, at long last, an earned wound and Sir Toby a bloody coxcomb. We don't see this second confrontation, in which Sebastian has apparently set upon the two knights in earnest. We have already enjoyed that joke, and Shakespeare apparently had no interest in giving his audience another display of Andrew's inept swordsmanship. He did, however, wish to exploit once again the confusion of identities between Sebastian and Viola. The entrance of Sir Andrew and Sir Toby provides a last instance of this before the recognition scene. They depart, with Andrew still pathetically trying to ingratiate himself: "I'll help you, Sir Toby, because we'll be dressed together,"—and Toby the picture of wounded irascibility: "Will you help—an ass-head and a cox-comb and a knave, a thin-fac'd knave, a gull!" (5.1.204–207).

The bested warriors exit, then, before Sebastian returns apologetically to the stage—"I am sorry, madam, I have hurt your kinsman" (209)—and they are thus denied the pleasure of the recognition scene. Shakespeare's motives for this early dismissal are not recoverable, though it may be more helpful to seek them in the realm of dramaturgy than in the realms of theme and meaning. For the next moments, with Fabian and Feste exiting as well to attend the brawlers, are extraordinarily intense. They seem best left to those who can respond to them most fully both with rich language and with silence. Sebastian comes at once to Olivia, but the first character to voice surprise is Orsino. Then Sebastian spies Antonio, who, beset by joy and puzzlement, asks, "Which is Sebastian?" (224). Only then does Olivia speak. Cued perhaps by a gesture implicit in Antonio's question, she looks at first one twin, then the other; and her words are as expressive as they are brief: "Most wonderful!" (225). These are her only words in the entire recognition episode (209–58), a testimony to Shakespeare's confidence in his actors, since Olivia (and Antonio, for that matter) must spend most of this episode in mute amazement and delight. Once again, the moment is full. In the theatre, no one witnessing the reunion of Viola and Sebastian will remark the absence of Sir Toby or Maria. Caught up in the magic of Shakespeare's stagecraft, and thus aware of the profound joy of the three onlookers even as the twins enumerate tokens of recognition, the spectators will "learn to read what silent love hath writ" (Son. 23.13).

It would have served this argument well if Shakespeare had stopped here at the point of union, with the matches made and his lovers in full accord. But Malvolio is brought to mind again when Viola, responding to Orsino's comically direct request—"let me see thee in thy woman's weeds"—explains that her garments are with the captain and that he "is now in durance, at Malvolio's suit" (273, 276). Olivia then recalls hearing of the steward's distraction and, distracted herself, gives the command to "fetch Malvolio hither" (278), although there is no servant on stage to respond to her order. She repeats it after Feste and Fabian enter and reveal to her Malvolio's complaining letter (315). Malvolio has a case; he has been abused, even "notoriously" so. But we should not forget that his dreams of grandeur are only enhanced by Maria's letter, not occasioned by it; and we should note, too, with Clifford Leech, that Malvolio's treatment of the captain seems introduced to justify our disapprobation.[11] Still, it would be easier if his famous exit and threat of revenge could be recognized for what it is, the last ineffectual gesture of a steward "sick of self-love." Then, echoing Maria, we might opt for flippant mockery—"Go shake your ears!" (2.3.125)—or, comparing small things to great, be even more icily dismissive: "That's but a trifle here" (Lr. 5.3.296). But a preference for one line of the stage tradition connection with Malvolio, the "tragic" reading that goes back to Lamb's account of Bensley, joined to recent critical emphasis on closure, has made the steward's role crucially important for interpretations of the play.[12]

The need to discuss Shakespeare's handling of Malvolio poses a critical dilemma, however, for a full response to previous critics would necessarily entail still further attention to his last appearance and thus further concentration on the play's close. One way to resolve this impasse may be to ask what dramatic needs remain after the recognition scene, or—better, perhaps—what dramatic needs Shakespeare attends to after that episode. He must, of course, deal with the question of Malvolio, but this does not mean that he has to solve a problem in human relations. Two assumptions seem to govern the view that Malvolio is a special instance. The first is that he has somehow been changed by his experience and that the abuse heaped upon him requires that we see him in a new light at the play's close. The second is that comedy ought to be subject to the laws of life rather than those of the stage. Both assumptions, I think, are misguided. Malvolio's character—composed of rigidity, officiousness, narcissism, self-righteousness, onanistic imaginings, and fundamental obtuseness—is not created by the maliciousness of those acting against him. It is simply there: in his contempt for Feste, his inability to cope with Orsino's witty messenger, his dream of having left Olivia sleeping, and his delivery of the ring, to mention only a few of the strokes that Shakespeare uses to sketch this brilliant portrait of "an affection'd ass" (2.3.148). At the close of the letter scene, spectators and readers alike join in the delight of the tricksters; and nothing later in the play, not even the admitted excesses of Malvolio's treatment in the dark room, is powerful enough to alter our view of his character or our acquiescence in his deception.

The Malvolio of Shakespeare's fifth act is no different from the Malvolio we have observed earlier in the play. He remains a rigid and uncompromising figure. Just as, earlier, he condemns others for their late-night license while he himself luxuriates in his imagination, leaving Olivia sleeping on a day-bed as he goes to rebuke Sir Toby, so here he finds himself "notoriously abused" by his treatment in a makeshift cell while the Captain suffers actual imprisonment. Despite this, other characters make an effort to mollify him, not only Olivia and Orsino but Fabian as well, who urges Olivia to

> let no quarrel, nor no brawl to come,
> Taint the condition of this present hour,
> Which I have wond'red at.
>
> (356–58)

Malvolio's exit, then, is of a piece with his behavior throughout the play, and it is therefore not merely accepted but almost predictable.

Still, the doubts remain. Is the specter of revenge not a fundamental threat to the Illyrian festivity launched so hopefully only moments before in the recognition episode? What sort of revenge will Malvolio attempt? Such questions are, I think, fundamentally irrelevant to the spirit of comic drama and our experience of the play. The issue here is merely a particular instance of a problem discussed earlier; and here, as there, I take the view that the world of the play is entire and whole, never dependent for its judgments on an appeal beyond its own terms and limitations.

Those terms, in *Twelfth Night*, seem to have required of Shakespeare one final task. The recognition scene belongs to Viola and Sebastian, though the other characters respond with wonder and, in so responding, focus our feelings as well. Now, in the play's last moments, Olivia and Orsino, its ranking figures, assume dominance. She introduces the question of Malvolio and, at his departure, agrees that "he hath been most notoriously abus'd" (379). Orsino makes the final judgment, accepting Olivia's view but imposing on the steward a responsibility as well:

> Pursue him, and entreat him to a peace;
> He hath not told us of the captain yet.
> (380–81)

In doing so, he fulfills the last necessity in Shakespeare's design. He assumes control, sending Fabian on his errand and conducting the final exit of the lovers. Fate and time having done their admirable work, Illyria's Duke assumes his proper role, no languishing synesthesiac but an authoritative and commanding figure, claiming with assurance his "mistress, and his fancy's queen" (388).

It remains for Feste to negotiate the play's final transaction, a movement away from the world of Illyria into the workaday world where spectators, denied access to the "golden time" anticipated by Orsino, must contend with the wind and the rain. Seen in this way, Feste's function hardly suggests that he should be "required to break down and sob in the course of his final song," as he was in one modern production.[13] His act of mediation here is but another illustration of Shakespeare's consistency and care in the design of *Twelfth Night*. Like other matters built on a detailed preparation, this bridge between the play world and the world of the audience fulfills or extends its pre-enactment. Throughout the play, Feste has moved between the two houses of Orsino and Olivia and the two plots—the romantic world of love in which Orsino has "unclasp'd / . . . the book even of [his] secret soul" and the heartier, more plainspoken world of Maria and Sir Toby, in which Maria is praised for being "as witty a piece of Eve's flesh as any in Illyria" (1.4.13–14, 1.5.27–28). Now he engages in a similar movement between two worlds, that of the play and that of the world outside the theatre. They are, he assures us, two quite different spheres. Summing up the song's account of growth, change, and misadventure, he appropriates Toby's favorite words of cavalier dismissal: "that's all one." Speaking as an actor assigned the task of encouraging our final applause, he tells us what we know: "our play is done." Acknowledging the players' dependence on their audience, he declares, "We'll strive to please you every day" (5.1.407–408).

Thus closure in *Twelfth Night,* far from being the key to interpretation and far from being problematic, is a dramatically skillful realization of connections prepared for and pre-enacted in the play's earlier events. It provides satisfaction not because it answers questions but because it presents the promised answers in such dramatically satisfying ways.

This reading of *Twelfth Night,* like all such readings, is necessarily incomplete. My hope is that it may serve not so much as a model of interpretation but as a signpost directing students of Shakespearean comedy to other forms of criticism that may take the burden off closure. My aim is not to deny comic endings their legitimate claim to importance. All sorts of issues, including the issue of genre itself, are tied up with questions of closure. Still, if the adage that "the end crowns the work" carries any implications, surely they have to do with fulfillment, expected results, natural succession. Crowning the end unseats those implications and, as with any usurpation, brings with it the likelihood of chaos.

Six

Comic Vitality and the Cost of Fantasy in *Measure for Measure*

he critical aggrandizement of closure, as my earlier discussions reveal, leads to difficulties and even distortions in the interpretation of Shakespeare's comedies. Among the problems resulting from such an emphasis, one might cite as especially prominent a lack of attention to short-term effects and a misleading stress on structure as a key to meaning. The latter critical strategy, which tends to see the plays as shaped by a teleological design, seems especially questionable when it gives rise to exclusivist readings urged by critics unwilling to tolerate the possibility of other views. In the case of the romantic comedies, we have seen that strikingly opposed attitudes toward individual plays could be advanced by critics who, in their explicit theorizing, placed equal emphasis on closure. Those who reject Frye and Barber and find in the plays darkness, discord, and other evidence of cynicism or dissatisfaction with the comic form nevertheless base their judgment on the same materials in which Frye and Barber discover clarification, a new ordering of society, and the impulse toward celebration.

Although *Measure for Measure* has its own critical history and one quite different from that of the Elizabethan comedies of Shakespeare (which is essentially a shared history, as John Russell Brown and others have pointed out),[1] the problems it exhibits and the points of attack chosen by its many critics are remarkably similar to those engendered by the romantic comedies. The chief difference is that the problems I am describing are primarily a matter of the last thirty years or so for the romantic comedies but a near-constant over the whole critical history of *Measure for Measure*. Thus while it is true that Northrop Frye, in a recent book entitled *The Myth of Deliverance,* enlarges his theory to accommodate the problem comedies, it is also the case that emphasis on closure has been a central feature of most of the approaches to *Measure for Measure* from early days.

What Frye argues is that *Measure for Measure* is a "fairly typical" comedy, one "in which redemptive forces are set to work that bring about the characteristic festive conclusion, the birth of a new society."[2] But earlier critics, led by their reliance on quite a diversity of patterns of meaning, had made essentially the same observation; and an equally impressive number of commentators, looking at the same evidence, arrived at quite contrary conclusions, seeing the play's ending as the final seal on a dramatic structure intended to be problematic and unsettling.

This division of opinion about *Measure for Measure,* and the dependence of writers on both sides on evidence drawn from the play's ending, should not be seen as invalidating my earlier argument about the importance of a Frye-Barber line of criticism and the opposition to that line. Much of the earlier criticism of *Measure for Measure* is character-based and only occasionally focused on comic structure. Moreover, the critics who find the romantic comedies problematic often see them as part of an evolutionary process (or evidence of a shift in Shakespeare's psychological outlook) leading to the uncertainty of *All's Well That Ends Well* and *Measure for Measure*. Thus the phylogeny of the romantic comedies' critical history is recapitulated in a more intense form in the ontogeny of critical approaches to *Measure for Measure*. Finally, and what matters most for my purpose here, *Measure for Measure* is a play whose closure has provided a compelling focus for critics of every persuasion. In their attention to its ending, and to its ending as an affirmation of meaning, the critics have sacrificed or ignored a great part of its theatrical life and comic richness.

Others have made this point about *Measure for Measure,* including Joan Rees in *Shakespeare and the Story* and, more recently, Harriet Hawkins. Rees attacks "over-intellectualizing and schematizing" critical approaches that "misrepresent the leaping life" of the plays; and Hawkins, defining the world of *Measure for Measure* as almost indescribably varied, argues that "in this teeming terrain—and not in an ending which appears to have tidied everything up—may lie the source of the play's vitality."[3] Before going on to my own effort at the elusive business of capturing some sense of the play's "leaping life," I want to take a moment or two to suggest why *Measure for Measure* seems especially amenable to schematic criticism of the sort deplored by Rees and Hawkins, and why such criticism seems invariably to focus on the play's ending as the point at which it asserts its meaning.

In a general way, these schematic approaches arise because the tendency of most criticism is toward order, even when it is contending with the most unruly and recalcitrant materials.[4] But in the case of *Measure for Measure* the play itself may be seen as encouraging a sort of absolutism in its interpretation, an absolutism that is reflected with disturbing consistency by the habit of reading it in a schematic way—i.e., subjecting it to systematic analysis dependent on materials outside itself—rather than responding to it.[5] The play's encouragement of such readings begins, of course, with its very title. The meting out of appropriate and exactly determined rewards and punishments, with all the quantitative precision implied in such a process, suggests one kind of absolutism. The title's significance on this level is supported throughout by references to devices of measurement, by the extensive use of words that concern precision and exactness, and by the staging of arguments that build on rigidly opposed and finally irreconcilable points of view. This tendency is reflected throughout the play:

> Thus can the demi-god, Authority,
> Make us pay down for our offense by weight.
> (1.2.120–21)

> We cannot weigh our brother with ourself.
> (2.2.126)

> If he had so offended,

> He would have weigh'd thy brother by himself.
> (5.1.110–11)

> by this is
> your brother sav'd, your honor untainted, the poor
> Mariana advantag'd, and the corrupt deputy scal'd.
> (3.1.253–55)

> He professes to have receiv'd no sinister measure from his judge.
> (3.2.242–43)

Since *Measure for Measure* reveals such an emphasis on weighing and assessing, and since it reiterates throughout its five acts a concern for exactitude in such matters, it seems as though the play itself calls for an interpretation that would be the product of such precise calculation. It would appear, that is, as though some abstract, schematic parabolic intention or some demonstrable ethical formula might provide the key to the meaning of this puzzling play. But to reason in such a fashion is to misread the evidence in a basic way and to be misled into using part of the problem as though it were the solution.

Measure for Measure is indeed filled with terms and images that suggest precision and exactitude, and its characters habitually think and argue in absolute terms. This absolutism, in tandem with the surface thematic concerns of the play—justice, vengeance and forgiveness, discovery and self-discovery—leads almost inevitably to a concern with the meanings that can be discovered in the play's close. If the Duke's purpose is to discover "what these seemers be," then his intention must wait upon the full revelation of Angelo's perfidy. If the play's thematic focus is justice, then our full understanding of its design can appear only when measure is given *for* measure; and in some readings this can occur only when Vincentio, doffing his friar's disguise, can assume the juridical role not merely of Duke but of "power divine." If the play is said to be about forgiveness rather than retribution, about grace rather than deserving, then its full significance appears only when Isabella kneels and "against all sense" joins Mariana in pleading for the life of Angelo.

Thus major elements in the play itself, joined to a widespread critical disposition to focus on closure, have made *Measure for Measure* especially susceptible to the sort of analysis that emphasizes teleology and, in effect, crowns the end.[6] In the discussion that follows, I want to recover something of what has been lost through that emphasis on closure and, in the process, suggest that close attention to frequently neglected moments in the comedy's development allows us to view the play's ending as far less problematic and troubling than it ordinarily seems to be.

Those who write about Shakespeare's plays know them so thoroughly—through constant rereading, teaching them year after year, occasional performances, and (most significantly) through the lenses of earlier critics—that it is almost impossible to get a new purchase on a single play or any of its characters. With characters especially we tend to read into their first appearance everything we know of them from previous knowledge (from whatever source); and we tend to read backward, attributing to those characters at their first appearance everything we have come to see only after the total experience of the play, including all the sources of interpretation and understanding available to us from outside the text.

Because we know, for example, that Quiller-Couch found Isabella "somewhat rancid in her chastity" and that R. W. Chambers saw her as exemplifying the greatest love in her willingness to "frankly, joyously, give her life to save Claudio."[7] Because we know that Isabella condemns her brother for his fearfulness and yet acts as the Duke's agent in gaining Mariana's assent to the bed trick. Because we know that Isabella proclaims, "more than our brother is our chastity" and then, at the play's close, apparently acquiesces without the slightest demurral to the Duke's desire to make her his wife. For these reasons and more, any effort to see Isabella and judge her behavior in an unbiased way is severely compromised. All this is only to say that, given the conditions under which criticism of Shakespeare goes forward, it is extraordinarily difficult to claim the helpful role of the naive spectator. But an effort to approach the play free from preconceptions (from whatever source) may earn substantial results, especially in coming to terms with its three main characters—Isabella, Angelo, and the Duke.

A key to Isabella's character—indeed, for some critics the very definition of her character—can be found in her special status as a novice. Visibly in most productions of the comedy and implicitly in most criticism, her costume remains an identifying mark of her character throughout the play. For many readers, this costume distinguishes her as, if not "a thing enskied, and sainted" (1.4.34), in Lucio's perhaps somewhat mocking terms, at least a figure whose commitment to holy orders plays a large role in her behavior toward both Angelo and her brother. Rosalind Miles qualifies this usual view by pointing out that "Isabella is the only young female of the drama of the period who is connected with the religious life in any significant way," and she goes on to suggest that some contemporary antireligious attitudes may allow for a comic dimension to the character. These "comic and derisive associations of her initial role . . . moderate our response," even if only to suggest "that Isabella is not to be taken by the audience quite as seriously as she takes herself."[8] This observation is on the right track, I think, though it is grounded on comparisons with other texts of the time and not on the language and theatrical possibilities provided in Shakespeare's play. What do those more immediate sources afford in the way of evidence for understanding Isabella?

Our first view of Isabella comes in 1.4, just before Lucio arrives on his embassy from Claudio. Bertrand Evans speaks of her as "frozen in nature" when she delivers her opening lines; J. W. Lever claims that "her first words in the scene, where as a one-day novice she calls for 'more strict restraint' in an ancient and austere order, suggest immature enthusiasm."[9] Her first words, however, are these, spoken to one who is presumably older and who is living according to the rigid and prescriptive rules of her order: "And have you nuns no farther privileges?" (1.4.1). The rest of this opening dialogue follows:

Fran. Are not these large enough?
Isab. Yes, truly; I speak not as desiring more,
But rather wishing a more strict restraint
Upon the sisterhood, the votarists of Saint Clare.

(2–5)

Isabella's first line is not enthusiastic at all.[10] At the most it is a request for information. If we see it as enthusiastic, it must mean something like "Do you really mean that the rules are just as tough as I've always heard? Wonderful!" This seems a forced and even improbable reading. If, on the other hand, we take it to mean something like "Is this all the freedom you have?" then what follows is quite understandable. The nun asks Isabella if the conditions of the order seem too harsh; and Isabella, well trained and anxious to please, disguises her disappointment with a hyperbolic statement of the exact contrary of her true feelings. Almost instinctively, she chooses her role—the enthusiastic novice—and delivers some pious lines appropriate to that role. The interruption of Lucio provides the occasion for yet more details about the order's precision, details offered up with a clipped rapidity of speech that suggests a nearly endless supply of such rote behavioral prescriptions suited to any and all situations:

> Turn you the key, and know his business of him;
> You may, I may not; you are yet unsworn.
> When you have vow'd, you must not speak with men
> But in the presence of the prioress;
> Then if you speak, you must not show your face,
> Or if you show your face, you must not speak.
> (1.4.8–13)

It should not surprise us, then, to hear a note of relief and even of childlike anticipation in Isabella's cry, "Peace and prosperity! Who is't that calls?" (15). Lucio's embassy succeeds in freeing Isabella from her rash and nearly reflexive embrace of a rigid and endlessly prescriptive religious order. But the same impulses that led her to ask for "a more strict restraint" as a poor Clare will cause her, in her encounters with Angelo and her brother, to adopt another and more dangerous moralistic role.

I want to return to Isabella's development later and shift now to Angelo in order to see how his initial appearance defines the basis on which Shakespeare will build his character. In the case of Isabella, our first view is conditioned by awareness of radically opposed critical views of her character and by apparent contradictions in her own behavior. In Angelo's case, our initial response is shaped by knowledge of his consistently reprehensible later behavior and by the virtual unanimity of critical opinion. The view of Coleridge still represents the consensus. He could not accept the fate Shakespeare assigns the absent Duke's deputy, his pardon and marriage to Mariana, "for cruelty, with lust and damnable baseness, cannot be forgiven, because we cannot conceive of them as being morally repented of."[11]

Given such weighty persuasions, it is almost impossible to regard Angelo without prejudice even at his first appearance. His merest polite response will be interpreted as sycophancy, and his reluctance to assume responsibility, far from being credited as understandable self-mistrust, will be seen as implicated in a line of imagery stressing deception and counterfeiting, the initial statement of the theme of the "fallen angel." In the theatre, such interpretations may give us an Angelo as aspiring Gestapo commander, clicking his heels as he bows:

> Always obedient to your Grace's will,
> I come to know your pleasure.
> (I.I.25–26)

Or they will present a less hard-edged character, one whose oleaginous self-deprecation makes him especially unattractive:

> Now, good my lord,
> Let there be some more test made of my mettle
> Before so noble and so great a figure
> Be stamp'd upon it.
> (I.I.47–50)

Either of these interpretations may work in the theatre, and both can be supported by reading backward from subsequent events or by applying certain general critical attitudes toward Angelo to his particular actions in this opening scene. But what the scene gives us is primarily the Duke (who speaks over three-quarters of its lines) announcing in rather cryptic language his intentions, passing over Escalus in favor of the youthful Angelo, and generally behaving in a way that underscores a haste so compelling "that it prefers itself, and leaves unquestion'd / Matters of needful value" (I.I.54–55). In this context, we are justified in seeing Angelo chiefly as confused, uncertain of his function, and no wiser than spectators or readers of the play about the Duke's mission. When Escalus, requesting a conference in order to clarify his puzzlement about the role he is to play, says, "A pow'r I have, but of what strength and nature / I am not yet instructed," Angelo can only share his uncertainty: " 'Tis so with me" (79-81). Shakespeare tells us nothing here of "seemers," nor do we have any warrant from the text for supposing that Angelo in this introductory scene must exhibit the arrogant use of power that later makes him so blameworthy in his conduct toward Isabella. If we are alert to Shakespeare's fondness for parallelism, we may see that Angelo, like Isabella, is being taken—by circumstances over which he has little control—from a relatively private and undemanding role to one that is both more public and more demanding.

Meanwhile, the Duke undertakes precisely the opposite journey, from a public role that he finds in some ways distasteful—"I love the people, / But do not like to stage me to their eyes" (1.1.67–68)—to a disguised existence that will allow him a closer and more disturbing view of a Vienna that has grown corrupt under his relatively lax administration. The Duke's appearance *in propria persona* in 1.1 does little more than set the plot in motion. His appearance in 1.3 clarifies the action of the earlier scene by suggesting a dual motivation for his departure: to reestablish discipline in the city and to test "Lord Angelo," who "scarce confesses / That his blood flows; or that his appetite / Is more to bread than stone" (50–53).

The Duke's friar disguise is a complicating feature of *Measure for Measure* on several grounds. It is, for example, firmly in the category of conventional theatrical tactics, and in nearly every case where conventional matters come into play in *Measure for Measure* they cause difficulty insofar as they collide with what critics judge to be the dominant realism of the comedy as a whole. Thus Harriet Hawkins, in a sort of catalogue of the structural infelicities that make closure in *Measure for Measure* so unsatisfying, points especially to the Duke's proposal of marriage to Isabella. Shakespeare, she says, "makes it come as a bolt from the blue" (105). The Duke's action is all the more surprising, she argues, in light of his assurance to Friar Thomas that no consideration of love could move him to adopt a disguise:

> No; holy father, throw away that thought;
> Believe not that the dribbling dart of love
> Can pierce a complete bosom.
>
> (1.3.1–3)

However we regard this denial, it has no status as evidence about the Duke's attitude toward women and should have no significant influence on our perception of his proposal to Isabella. In some ways, the Duke's disclaimer is most satisfactorily seen as one stage in the life cycle of a convention, that of the disguised ruler, widely current in Renaissance drama and seen in such plays as Marston's *The Fawn*, Middleton's *The Phoenix*, and Beaumont's *The Woman-Hater*.[12]

For the naive spectator, though, such conventions can have no more effect on his perceptions of the Duke than can the knowledge of future events within the play: the Duke's machinations in arranging the bed trick, for example, or his offer of marriage to Isabella. All such a spectator has to go on at this point are the Duke's professed intentions and perhaps a general sense that disguise of any sort is a likely prelude to trouble for the disguiser. Each of the play's major figures, then, moves into the second act encountering a new world: for Isabella, the world of ubiquitous and aggressive sexuality outside the convent; for Angelo, the world of power and political manipulation available to those in the seats of authority; and for the Duke, the teeming underworld of Vienna that has grown corrupt under his ineffective rule.

It seems almost willfully incorrect, therefore, to speak of these characters' subsequent behavior as the product of deep conviction or ingrained habit. Rather, the action of *Measure for Measure*, like that of many dramas of intrigue, is largely a matter of improvisation, adaptation to rapidly shifting circumstances, and responses generated less from principle than from unexpectedly emergent challenges and opportunities. This being so, it is more surprising still that critics have been at such pains to fit all the elements of the play into a coherent and purposive design whose meanings are discovered only in its ending.[13]

In large part, *Measure for Measure* may even be said to be about *resistance* to design. What Angelo is attempting through his imposition of strict legality, what the convent's rules represent, what the Duke so conspicuously failed at, all suggest an effort to control and direct human nature. In the course of the play, various elements of society and particular figures challenge that effort and seem to suggest an elemental antagonism to such attempts at constraint. Lucio is the most striking figure here, but Mistress Overdone, Pompey, and Barnardine all perform the same function. Theodore Spencer once wrote that around the turn of the century in 1600 there was no question more widely discussed than "What is the nature of man?"[14] Today, he would probably have corrected that observation to suggest the inclusion of women, and there is no doubt that as the century opened such plays as *The Widow's Tears, Sophonisba,* and *The Dutch Courtesan* made the issue applicable to both sexes. But it is clear that for Shakespeare it is central throughout his career (and not merely around the time of *Hamlet*)—from *Love's Labor's Lost,* with its repudiation of the courtiers' life-denying commitment to "war against [their] own affections / And the huge army of the world's desires" (1.1.9–10), to *The Tempest,* where Ariel instructs Prospero ("Mine would, sir, were I human" [5.1.20]) in the need to renounce vengeance in order to pursue his higher nature.

Shakespeare wastes no time before acquainting us with this fundamental opposition between the forces of nature and those who would restrict them. As Angelo and Escalus make their exit in 1.1 to consult about the "strength and nature" of their power, Lucio and the two gentlemen enter to begin 1.2 in an atmosphere of self-important political analysis, gossip, and bawdy repartee. The dramatic strategy here is Shakespeare's familiar use of anonymous marginal figures to provide insight into the play world from an outsider's perspective. In *Richard III* the citizens in 2.3 serve this function; in *Richard II,* the gardener and his man. But here the difference is that these figures represent a force in life that, unable to escape marginalization, will nevertheless persist in living on the margins according to its own lights, ungoverned finally by rules imposed by a central authority.

Lucio's account of "the sanctimonious pirate, that went to sea with the Ten Commandements, but scrap'd one out of the table" (7–9) is thus no riddle to his companions. The second gentleman instinctively knows that the "raz'd" injunction was " 'Thou shalt not steal,' " and his fellow defends the pirate's action: "Why, 'twas a commandement to command the captain and all the rest from their functions; they put forth to steal. There's not a soldier of us all, that in the thanksgiving before meat, do relish the petition well that prays for peace" (1.2.12–16). It is this same wisdom, resistant to control and endlessly adaptive, that Pompey invokes to console Mistress Overdone when she wails, "here's a change indeed in the commonwealth! What shall become of me?" "Come," says Pompey, "fear not you; good counsellors lack no clients. Though you change your place, you need not change your trade" (1.2.104-108).

Throughout the play, versions of this theme recur with striking insistence. Pompey's masterful evasiveness in the hearing before Escalus finally drives that official to an outburst of impatience: "Which is the wiser here: Justice or Iniquity?" (2.1.172). Lucio, arguing to the disguised Duke that Angelo might display "a little more lenity to lechery," goes on to declare that "the vice is of a great kindred; it is well allied; but it is impossible to extirp it quite, friar, till eating and drinking be put down" (3.2.97, 101-103). At the most elemental level, the idea is repeated yet again when Barnardine—"He is coming, sir, he is coming. I hear his straw rustle"—enters to assert his resistance to the law's requirement: "I have been drinking hard all night, and I will have more time to prepare me, or they shall beat out my brains with billets. I will not consent to die this day, that's certain" (4.3.35–36, 53–56).

It seems important to note that this attitude of resistance to imposed authority, through evasion or flat-out denial, unites nearly all the low characters in the play—unites all those, that is, who represent the underground life of the city of Vienna. They speak for, and they act out the needs of, those who would respond to nature and follow its promptings. To deny these citizens their freedom (and I take it that sexual freedom is only a figure here for all sorts of impulses toward a full life) would require radical and ultimately unacceptable measures. Thus Pompey, in response to Escalus's tautological assertion that the trade of bawd is not lawful because "the law will not allow it," answers with a chilling question: "Does your worship mean to geld and splay all the youth of the city?" (2.1.228, 230–31). This emphasis on the life of the city validates, in my view, those productions of *Measure for Measure* that make an effort to present the whole of Vienna, to show us the reality that in their various ways Angelo, Isabella, and the Duke try to ignore. And it gives another justification for the sort of "public resolution" that Bernard Beckerman speaks of in discussing the play's final scene.[15] But that does not signify that closure in *Measure for Measure* is the key to meaning; indeed, those critical readings that find the play's chief meaning in its close are able to do so only through a reductionism that "gelds and splays" the comedy itself.

The broadest forms of that comedy appear, of course, in the scenes involving the play's low characters; and since those scenes are often neglected in discussions of *Measure for Measure*, it may be helpful at this point to consider them. The first of them, 1.2, reflects in a general way some familiar elements of Shakespeare's stagecraft: a shift from a high level of action and discourse to a low, a serial introduction of low comic characters, a rapid unfolding of plot, and the introduction through description of a female character whose special qualities are made so vivid that spectators are keyed to her eventual appearance. Beyond those familiar elements and dominating them, as he dominates the comic tone of the whole play, is the figure of Lucio. His very entrance is a sign of discord. Escalus closes the previous scene deferring to Angelo—"I'll wait upon your honor" (84)—and Lucio, hardly the theme of honor's tongue, enters with his brash, know-it-all analysis of the political scene.[16]

In the theatre, the word *honor* still fills the air as Lucio and the two gentlemen begin their bout of raillery. Their talk, with its subjects of thieving, corruption, and sexual infection, reflects the unwholesomeness of the city itself and is essentially negative and derogatory. Even their mention of grace introduces that notion in a negative way. Lucio's assertion—"Grace is grace, despite of all controversy; as, for example, thou thyself art a wicked villain, despite of all grace" (1.2.24–26)—contrasts interestingly with the more famous passage in *Macbeth*: "Though all things foul would wear the brows of grace, / Yet grace must still look so" (4.3.23–24). In the tragic context, the idea of grace is held out as immutable and enduring; in the comic context, it is seen as ineffectual when pitted against confirmed villainy.

But the reference to grace ought not to be taken as sounding a thematic note. Like much of this scene, its chief effect is to display Lucio as an irrepressible jokester, self-important and cocksure, insistent on getting the best of any verbal exchange. Throughout 1.2 Shakespeare settles him in this role: Lucio controls the stage and those who share it with him—"Behold, behold, where Madame Mitigation comes" (45); "Away! Let's go learn the truth of it" (81)—and makes even the plight of Claudio the occasion of jesting. To the unhappy prisoner's analysis of his faults, Lucio jokes, "If I could speak so wisely under an arrest, I would send for certain of my creditors" (131–32), suggesting, I suppose, that such eloquence might gain him remission of some sort.

It is not surprising that Lucio's deflating comment has been so little attended to by critics. Claudio's "speech" is more to their purpose. High-sounding, striking in its central metaphor, it seems to analyze the excesses of the city even as it defines Claudio's self-awareness. His restraint, he tells Lucio, comes from "too much liberty"; and

> As surfeit is the father of much fast,
> So every scope by the immoderate use
> Turns to restraint. Our natures do pursue,
> Like rats that ravin down their proper bane,
> A thirsty evil, and when we drink we die.
> (126–30)

But a theatre audience, keyed in to Lucio's conduct of the scene, is likely to attend chiefly to his mockery, judging Claudio's remarks in light of the fool's cynical response. And it is just in this function that we may see Lucio as one of the company of Shakespeare's fools, sometimes (like Feste) ingratiating but with a spirit of sly mockery, sometimes (like Lear's fool) pointing to motivations and even behaviors that his betters cannot call by their right names.

The rest of this initial scene of clowning has two major functions beyond presenting Lucio. First is the introduction of Mistress Overdone and Pompey, who embody the excesses the Duke means to purge through the agency of Angelo; second, and emerging from the first, is the establishment of Claudio's situation, with Angelo as principal cause and Isabella as sole hope for pardon. Since these two matters are so bound up with one another, it seems inevitable that Claudio's plight (and our perception of his case) should be tinged with comedy. We learn of his desperate situation first, in fact, in the context of a discussion of venereal disease and a bawdy exchange of insults. To Lucio's taunt—"Thy bones are hollow; impiety has made a feast of thee"—the first gentleman replies in kind: "How now, which of your hips has the most profound sciatica?" (56–59).[17] Then Mistress Overdone halts the slanging match with her news:

> Mrs. Ov. Well, well, there's one yonder arrested and carried to prison was worth five thousand of you all.

2. Gent. Who's that, I pray thee?
Mrs. Ov. Marry, sir, that's Claudio, Signior Claudio.
1. Gent. Claudio to prison? 'tis not so.
Mrs. Ov. Nay, but I know 'tis so. I saw him arrested; saw him carried away; and which is more, within these three days his head to be chopp'd off.

(60–69)

Claudio's statement of his difficulties (145–55), while not in itself comic, exhibits a sort of evasiveness that often seems to transform excuses into evidence of guilt. When he brings matters to a periphrastic conclusion—"it chances / The stealth of our most mutual entertainment / With character too gross is written on Juliet"—Lucio punctuates Claudio's euphemism with the obvious and deflating question: "With child, perhaps?" (156). And even as Claudio commissions Lucio to secure Isabella's intercession—a charge itself made somewhat equivocal by his use of *assay, prone, move,* and *play*—Lucio responds in a way that further lightens the atmosphere.[18] To Claudio's assurance that his sister "hath prosperous art / When she will play with reason and discourse, / And well she can persuade" (184–86), Lucio's response is characteristically self-concerned and irreverent: "I pray she may; as well for the encouragement of the like, which else would stand under grievous imposition, as for the enjoying of thy life, who I would be sorry should be thus foolishly lost at a game of tick-tack" (187–91).

Lucio's promise to return "within two hours" suggests a source of hope for Claudio that in the event will be blasted. The next scene offers yet another source of assurance in the person of the Duke, who is settling on the matter of his disguise with Friar Thomas. Together these elements provide something like a distancing effect that enables spectators to take Claudio's situation far less seriously than they might otherwise do. As the comedy unfolds, and as Isabella's hoped-for assistance turns to its opposite through the agency of Angelo's wickedness, Claudio's situation becomes increasingly filled with menace. As in the familiar paradox of Brecht's alienation effect, Shakespeare's care to distance us from serious emotional concern is defeated in large measure by the skill of his writing. Nevertheless, the comic strain in *Measure for Measure* is rarely absent for long; and Shakespeare never fails to keep his spectators aware of other perspectives on events that seem to his characters wholly distressing.[19]

One means of doing that, of course, is through the use of mirror scenes of the sort described by Hereward Price and understood by all subsequent students of Shakespeare as a central feature of his stagecraft.[20] In *Measure for Measure,* 2.1 offers a textbook example of such a scene. Elbow, haling "two notorious benefactors" before Angelo and Escalus, does more than offer a reprise of Dogberry, though he shares that inept constable's unerring penchant for the wrong word. In charging Pompey and Froth with misdeeds, Elbow manages to provide only the sketchiest details of their wrongdoing but in the process implicates his wife in shenanigans at the "hot-house" operated by Mistress Overdone since her earlier establishment was "pluck'd down in the suburbs." Like Angelo, then, the bumbling constable ends up tainting himself through his own efforts to enforce the law. Even Escalus cannot escape being touched by the bawdiness of subject and discourse here. His impatient urging of Pompey, "Come to me what was done to her," gets converted by the bawd into a sexual innuendo: "your honor cannot come to that yet"; "Sir, but you shall come to it" (118–19, 121).

While those who represent the law in 2.1 are being touched by vices they mean to reprehend and punish, the very notion of the law itself is being overturned. The scene as a whole stands as a comic version of Lear's "handy-dandy." After Angelo's exit (138), what began as a judicial inquiry degenerates into a farce of charge and countercharge, with the quarrel between Pompey and Elbow given additional ironic point by the exasperation of Escalus and the laconic responses of the witless Froth. When Escalus cries, "Which is the wiser here, Justice or Iniquity?" the immediate cause of his outburst is clear enough; it is the inane argument over whether Elbow's wife has been a "respected" person, and if so, with whom. This wonderful silliness, with Pompey taking up Elbow's verbal blunders for his own amusement, continues beyond Escalus's comically anguished question in Elbow's sputtering and impotent rage:

> O thou caitiff! O thou varlet! O thou wicked Hannibal! I respected with her before I was married to her? If ever I was respected with her,

> or she with me, let not your worship think me the poor Duke's officer. Prove this, thou wicked Hannibal, or I'll have mine action of batt'ry on thee.
>
> (174–79)

But the outcome of all this, as a judicial process, is remarkable for its inconsequence or perhaps for its reversal of expectations. Pompey is given a warning not to appear before the authorities again. But while he thanks Escalus for his "good counsel," he informs the audience in an aside of his true intentions: "but I shall follow it as the flesh and fortune shall better determine"(253–54). Then Escalus turns to Elbow, and in a masterly display of diplomacy lays the groundwork for removing the constable from his job:

> Escal. Come hither to me, Master Elbow; come hither, Master Constable. How long have you been in this place of constable?
> Elb. Seven year and a half, sir.
> Escal. I thought, by the readiness in the office, you had continu'd in it some time. You say seven years together?
> Elb. And a half, sir.
> Escal. Alas, it hath been great pains to you. They do you wrong to put you so oft upon't. Are there not men in your ward sufficient to serve it?
> Elb. Faith, sir, few of any wit in such matters. As they are chosen, they are glad to choose me for them. I do it for some piece of money, and go through with all.
> Escal. Look you bring me in the names of some six or seven, the most sufficient of your parish.
> Elb. To your worship's house, sir?
> Escal. To my house. Fare you well.
>
> (257–75)[21]

The whole of 2.1, then, providing as it does our first view of the system of justice under Angelo's administration, disposes us to see not harshness but ineptitude. Escalus's admonition to Pompey seems as ineffectual as it is wordy:

> Thank you, good Pompey; and in requital of your prophecy, hark you: I advise you let me not find you before me again upon any complaint whatsoever; no, not for dwelling where you do. If I do, Pompey, I shall beat you to your tent, and prove a shrewd Caesar to you; in plain-dealing, Pompey, I shall have you whipt. So for this time, Pompey, fare you well.
>
> (244–51)

Moreover, the bawd's response illustrates how little touched he is by threats of future punishment:

> Whip me? No, no, let carman whip his jade,
> The valiant heart's not whipt out of his trade.
> (255–56)

Taken alone, this scene comments tellingly on the play's treatment of such issues as justice, repentance, and reform. Taken in conjunction with other episodes that call the notion of "measure for measure" into question, it encourages a view of the play that sees its close as neither problematic nor celebratory but as fundamentally ironic and therefore consonant with the overall tone and structure of the play. Again and again, episodes in *Measure for Measure* begin with a clear purpose and end with that purpose overturned and frustrated.

The outcome of 2.1, with Pompey released and Elbow slated for early dismissal, is only the first of such episodes. Others would include Pompey's subsequent arrest and his appointment as apprentice executioner to Abhorson, Barnardine's refusal to accept judgment and the providential death of Ragozine, and Lucio's final descent into marriage with Kate Keepdown after his strenuous efforts to ally himself with the socially superior persons of the play. On another level of significance, the same pattern appears in Isabella's pleading to Claudio, which leads to her victimization and greater pressure for her brother's death; in Angelo's accession to power, which leads to the overthrow of his principles and recognition of a "sensual race" he had formerly controlled; and in the Duke's disguising, which exposes him to the calumny of Lucio and nearly opens the way for the rape of Isabella, the death of Claudio, and the total corruption of the deputy Angelo.

In each of the three instances just mentioned, the actions of Isabella, Angelo, and the Duke, it is possible to discern again a pattern of frustrated and overthrown intentions. Significantly, though, what one might think of as reasonable and praiseworthy aims in the actions involving the lower characters become here unrealistic and dangerous proceedings. Each of the three main characters, in fact, can be seen as acting out a fantasy role. Isabella, whose initial appearance shows her welcoming an unexpected release from a life choice she has found unsuitable, leaps immediately to another. Removed from the world and protected from its incitements to appetite, she enters it again in a context that exposes her to extreme sexual and psychological pressure. From a fantasy of escapism, she turns to a fantasy of heroic resistance. Angelo, too, takes on a fantasy role: given command in the Duke's absence, he imagines that "he is indeed Justice" and indulges himself in the fantasy that he may experience unlimited power. The Duke, perhaps even more seriously misled, allows himself the fantasy of believing that his disguise will allow him the exercise of power without responsibility.

Ultimately, however, these roles prove unsupportable. Each of them involves an absolute identity—unequivocal, and perfect in its simplicity. But human character is never static; it responds to new situations and new relationships, and it adapts to the demands imposed by forces over which it has no control. In their fantasy roles, the central figures of *Measure for Measure* confront the human problems presented to them with a degree of certainty possible only to those who have no choices to make. Paradoxically, it can be said that their free choice of roles has left them without freedom. Eventually, however, the characters are forced out of their fantasy roles. First the Duke, who must take up the reins of power behind the scenes when he recognizes the devastation and injustice that threaten in Angelo's willful exercise of power. Next Isabella, whose only escape from her intolerable dilemma lies in cooperation with the Duke's elaborate plotting. And finally Angelo, who persists in his abuse of power up to the very point at which the Duke reveals himself.

Dorothy Parker once wrote a story called "The Standard of Living." It may seem a most unlikely source for aid in understanding *Measure for Measure*, but as a sort of parable it may be instructive. The story is familiar, and here I wish to sketch only its barest outlines. Two New York office workers spend many of their leisure hours playing a version of the game "If I Had a Million Dollars." They play it with great earnestness and with rules that tend to make it a serious affair. One day, caught up in the fantasy of the game, they spy in a jeweler's window a most beautiful and opulent double strand of pearls. On a dare, they enter to inquire the price. The clerk, in the most matter-of-fact way, tells them: two hundred and fifty thousand dollars. The shock hits with a terrible effect, but after some uncertain moments one of the young women recovers:

> Look. Suppose there was this terribly rich person, see? You don't know this person, but this person has seen you somewhere and wants to do something for you. Well, it's a terribly old person, see? And so this person dies, just like going to sleep, and leaves you ten million dollars. Now what would be the first thing you'd do?[22]

Something like this happens in *Measure for Measure*. The characters are forced out of their fantasy roles, but with the difference, of course, that they are not permitted to take up the game again. When the time for evaluation comes, the judgments proceed in the midst of life.

Like life's own judgments, those made at the close of *Measure for Measure* are provisional and contingent. If the Duke's arrangements seem fragile and imperfect, they are at least consistent in that respect with other such efforts to control society and its constituents that we have witnessed earlier in the play. It is no wonder, then, that so many critics have found the play lacking when they ask that Shakespeare supply it with a satisfactory comic ending or, conversely, when they look to it for a severe justice answerable to the malicious intentions of Angelo. Neither of these endings fits the play Shakespeare wrote. As in the earlier comedies I have discussed, Shakespeare seems reluctant to have the ending of *Measure for Measure* assume the burden of creating both effective closure and a locus of meaning. Instead, in its ending the play recapitulates a pattern observed at several points in its unfolding. As it manifests itself in the comedy's closing moments, that pattern provides us with a sense of incompleteness that is one hallmark of satire.[23] If that seems less than we desire, we must accept that Shakespeare, in the play he wrote, promises us no more.

Notes

One. Crowning the End

1. John Russell Brown, "The Interpretation of Shakespeare's Comedies: 1900–1953," *Shakespeare Survey* 8 (1955): 1–13, p. 7.

2. Wayne A. Rebhorn, "After Frye: A Review-Article on the Interpretation of Shakespearean Comedy and Romance," *Texas Studies in Language and Literature* 21 (1979): 553–82, p. 533.

3. Samuel Johnson, "Preface to Shakespeare," *Johnson on Shakespeare*, ed. Arthur Sherbo, vol. 7, the Yale Edition of the Works of Samuel Johnson, ed. E. L. McAdam, Jr., et al. (New Haven: Yale UP, 1968), p. 72.

4. John Dover Wilson, *Shakespeare's Happy Comedies* (London: Faber and Faber, 1962), p. 36.

5. Frye's influence dates from as early as 1948, with the publication of "The Argument of Comedy," *English Institute Essays 1948*, ed. D. A. Robertson, Jr. (New York: Columbia UP, 1949, 58–73), and has continued, in such works as *The Anatomy of Criticism* (Princeton: Princeton UP, 1957) and *A Natural Perspective* (New York: Columbia UP, 1965). Barber's contribution is, of course, *Shakespeare's Festive Comedy* (1959; Princeton: Princeton UP, 1972).

6. Alexander Pope, "An Essay on Criticism," I, 73.

7. Norman Rabkin, *Shakespeare and the Problem of Meaning* (Chicago: U of Chicago P, 1981).

8. Interestingly, Frye uses the term *teleological* to contrast Jonson's comedy to Shakespeare's. But it seems clear that in the ordinary significance of the word it describes the approach to the comedies taken by Barber as well as by Frye.

9. Ralph Berry, *Shakespeare's Comedies: Explorations in Form* (Princeton: Princeton UP, 1972), p. 13.

10. Elliot Krieger, *A Marxist Study of Shakespeare's Comedies* (Totowa, N.J.: Barnes and Noble, 1979), p. 125.

11. Anthony B. Dawson, *Indirections: Shakespeare and the Art of Illusion* (Toronto: U of Toronto P, 1978), p. xii.

12. See Joseph Summers, "The Masks of *Twelfth Night*," *University of Kansas City Review* 22 (1955): 25–32.

13. Philip Edwards, *Shakespeare and the Confines of Art* (London: Methuen, 1968).

14. W. Thomas MacCary, *Friends and Lovers: The Phenomenology of Desire in Shakespearean Comedy* (New York: Columbia UP, 1985), p. 79.

15. William C. Carroll, *The Metamorphoses of Shakespearean Comedy* (Princeton: Princeton UP, 1985), p. 31.

16. See Blaze Bonazza, *Shakespeare's Early Comedies: A Structural Analysis*, Studies in English Literature 9 (The Hague: Mouton, 1966); Charles R. Lyons, *Shakespeare and the Ambiguity of Love's Triumph*, Studies in English Literature 68 (The Hague: Mouton, 1971); Patrick Swindon, *An Introduction*

to Shakespeare's Comedies (London: Macmillan, 1973); and Leo Salingar, *Shakespeare and the Traditions of Comedy* (Cambridge: Cambridge UP, 1974). Rebhorn's analysis is more detailed than mine and more judgmental, as is appropriate in a review essay. He does not see Frye and Barber as I do, for he finds Barber far less concerned with structure than Frye, more interested in tone and mood.

17. Edward Berry, *Shakespeare's Comic Rites* (Cambridge: Cambridge UP, 1984), p. ix.

18. A. P. Riemer, *Antic Fables: Patterns of Evasion in Shakespeare's Comedies* (New York: St. Martin's, 1980), p. 10.

19. Jan Kott, *Shakespeare Our Contemporary*, trans. Boleslaw Taborski, 2nd ed. (London: Methuen, 1967), p. 323.

20. Clifford Leech, Twelfth Night *and Shakespearean Comedy* (Toronto: Dalhousie UP, 1965), p. 38.

21. Thomas Van Laan, *Role-Playing in Shakespeare* (Toronto: U of Toronto P, 1978), p. 84

22. Richard A. Levin, *Love and Society in Shakespearean Comedy* (Newark: U of Delaware P, 1985), pp. 20, 215.

23. The attention given to closure in discussions of Shakespearean comedy is not at all an isolated phenomenon. Barbara Herrnstein Smith and Frank Kermode are perhaps the most conspicuous and influential among critics who have focused on the issue of closure in other genres. See Smith, *Poetic Closure: A Study of How Poems End* (Chicago: U of Chicago P, 1968), and Kermode, *The Sense of an Ending* (New York: Oxford UP, 1967).

24. Peter Erickson, *Patriarchal Structures in Shakespeare's Drama* (Berkeley and Los Angeles: U of California P, 1985). It should be obvious that there are certain critical practices that do not work within the terms I am using here. "One of the many lessons to be learned from Derrida's . . . practice of reading and writing," says David Hult, "is that the temporality and topology of the text are such that it is impossible to disentangle its literary and philosophical moments." If this position is accepted, then obviously the notion of closure as critical concept is rendered all but useless. For an extended discussion of this issue from a variety of viewpoints, see *Concepts of Closure*, Yale French Studies 67 (1984), ed. David Hult, from which the quotation just cited is taken (22). It is also obvious that for most writers on Shakespeare's comedies the concepts of closure and ending are not merely viable but essential to their understanding of how the plays work.

25. Marilyn Williamson, *The Patriarchy of Shakespeare's Comedies* (Detroit: Wayne State UP, 1986).

26. Adrian Louis Montrose, " 'The Place of a Brother' in *As You Like It*: Social Process and Comic Form," *Shakespeare Quarterly* 32 (1981): 28–54. I discuss the work of Montrose and Erickson, and to a lesser extent that of Williamson, in my chapter on *As You Like It*, when I elaborate on the point made here.

27. R. S. White, *Shakespeare and the Romance Ending* (Newcastle: Tyneside Free P, 1981), p. 23.

28. Ben Jonson, *Epicoene, or, The Silent Woman*, ed. L. A. Beaurline, Regents Renaissance Drama Series (Lincoln: U of Nebraska P, 1966), 5.4.195.

29. Jonson, *Volpone, or, The Fox,* ed. R. B. Parker, The Revels Plays (Manchester: Manchester UP, 1983), p. 75.

30. Robert Green, *Friar Bacon and Friar Bungay,* ed. Daniel Seltzer, Regents Renaissance Drama Series (Lincoln: U of Nebraska P, 1963), p. 94.

31. Richard L. Levin, *New Readings vs. Old Plays: Recent Trends in the Reinterpretation of English Renaissance Drama* (Chicago: U of Chicago P, 1979).

32. Joseph A. Bryant, Jr., *Shakespeare and the Uses of Comedy* (Lexington: UP of Kentucky, 1986), p. 84.

33. A. D. Moody, *Shakespeare:* The Merchant of Venice (London: Edward Arnold, 1964), p. 10.

34. Nevill Coghill, "The Basis of Shakespearean Comedy," *Essays and Studies* 3 (1950): 23.

35. Frank Kermode, "The Mature Comedies," *Early Shakespeare,* Stratford-upon-Avon Studies 3, ed. John Russell Brown and Bernard Harris (London: Edward Arnold, 1961), pp. 220–21.

36. Anne Barton, "*As You Like It* and *Twelfth Night*: Shakespeare's Sense of an Ending," *Shakespearian Comedy,* Stratford-upon-Avon Studies 14, ed. Malcolm Bradbury and David Palmer (London: Edward Arnold, 1972), p. 167. Barton employs ideas developed by Frank Kermode in *The Sense of an Ending.*

37. Alexander Leggatt, *Shakespeare's Comedy of Love* (London: Methuen, 1974), p. xi.

38. See, for example, John Russell Brown, *Shakespeare's Dramatic Style*: Romeo and Juliet, As You Like It, Julius Caesar, Twelfth Night, Macbeth (London: Heinemann, 1970), and John L. Styan, *Shakespeare's Stagecraft* (Cambridge: Cambridge UP, 1967).

39. Bernard Beckerman, *Shakespeare at the Globe* (New York: Columbia UP, 1962), p. 39.

40. Zvi Jagendorf, *The Happy End of Comedy: Jonson, Molière, and Shakespeare* (Newark: U of Delaware P, 1984), p. 1.

41. Thomas Kyd, *The Spanish Tragedy,* ed. Phillip Edwards, The Revels Plays (Cambridge: Harvard UP, 1959), 2.6.8 and note.

Two. "A wild of nothing, save of joy"

1. Samuel Johnson, "Preface to Shakespeare," *Johnson on Shakespeare,* ed. Arthur Sherbo, vol. 7, the Yale Edition of the Works of Samuel Johnson, ed. E. L. McAdam, Jr., et al., 14 vols. (New Haven: Yale UP, 1958), p. 69.

2. John Russell Brown, "The Interpretation of Shakespeare's Comedies: 1900–1953," *Shakespeare Survey* 8 (1955): 1–13; Northrop Frye, "The Argument of Comedy," *English Institute Essays 1948,* ed. D. A. Robertson, Jr. (New York: Columbia UP, 1949); *The Anatomy of Criticism: Four Essays* (Princeton: Princeton UP, 1957); *A Natural Perspective: The Development of Shakespearean Comedy and Romance* (New York: Columbia UP, 1965); C. L. Barber, *Shakespeare's Festive Comedy: A Study of Dramatic Form and Its Relation to Social Custom* (1959; Princeton: Princeton UP, 1972).

3. Stephen Fender, *Shakespeare:* A Midsummer Night's Dream (London: Edward Arnold, 1968), p. 30.

4. D. Allen Carroll and Gary J. Williams, eds., A Midsummer Night's Dream: *An Annotated Bibliography* (New York: Garland, 1986), p. x.

5. Anne Barton, "Shakespeare's Sense of an Ending in *Twelfth Night,*" Twelfth Night: *Critical Essays*, ed. Stanley Wells (New York: Garland, 1986), p. 309.

6. Alexander Leggatt, *Shakespeare's Comedy of Love* (London: Methuen, 1974), p. 254.

7. Ruth Nevo, *Comic Transformations in Shakespeare* (London: Methuen, 1980), p. 215.

8. Leo Salingar, "The Design of *Twelfth Night,*" Twelfth Night: *Critical Essays*, ed. Stanley Wells (New York: Garland, 1986), p. 212.

9. Norman Rabkin, *Shakespeare and the Problem of Meaning* (Chicago: U of Chicago P, 1981).

10. Joseph A. Bryant, Jr., *Shakespeare and the Uses of Comedy* (Lexington: UP of Kentucky, 1986), p. 84.

11. A. D. Moody, *Shakespeare:* The Merchant of Venice (London: Edward Arnold, 1964).

12. Lawrence Danson, *The Harmonies of* The Merchant of Venice (New Haven: Yale UP, 1978).

13. John B. Shackford, "The Bond of Kindness: Shylock's Humility," *University of Kansas City Review*, Winter 1954, pp. 85–91.

14. Richard L. Levin, *New Readings vs. Old Plays: Recent Trends in the Reinterpretation of English Renaissance Drama* (Chicago: U of Chicago P, 1979), p. 204.

15. Bertrand Evans, *Shakespeare's Comedies* (Oxford: Oxford UP, 1960).

16. The character was played in the broadest possible terms, making Morocco appear like one of the lodge brothers from "Amos 'n' Andy" dressed in a costume party getup of turban and robe.

17. J. L. Styan, *Shakespeare's Stagecraft* (Cambridge: Cambridge UP, 1967), p. 134.

18. Many commentators claim that Belmont, no less than Venice, adheres chiefly to commercial values. James Shapiro's comment suggests how far this view has become today's critical orthodoxy: "As critics increasingly realize, Belmont is much more like Venice than it would like to acknowledge; the distinctions between the two worlds, nervously insisted upon by Belmont, begin to collapse." See " 'Which Is *The Merchant* Here, and Which *The Jew*?': Shakespeare and the Economics of Influence," *Shakespeare Studies* 20 (1988): 275.

19. See Hereward T. Price, "Mirror Scenes in Shakespeare," *Joseph Quincy Adams Memorial Studies*, ed. James G. McManaway et al. (Washington, D.C.: The Folger Shakespeare Library, 1948), pp. 101–13, and David P. Young, *Something of Great Constancy: The Art of* A Midsummer Night's Dream (New Haven: Yale UP, 1966), pp. 97–106.

20. William Shakespeare, *The Merchant of Venice*, The Arden Shakespeare, ed. John Russell Brown (London: Methuen, 1955), p. lviii.

Three. "The Career of . . . Humor"

1. William Shakespeare, *Much Ado about Nothing*, The Arden Shakespeare, ed. A. R. Humphreys (London: Methuen, 1981), 5.4.126n.

2. See Barber, *Shakespeare's Festive Comedy: A Study of Dramatic Form and Its Relation to Social Custom* (1959; Princeton: Princeton UP, 1972), p. 222; Frye, *A Natural Perspective: The Development of Shakespearean Comedy and Romance* (New York: Columbia UP, 1965), p. 81; and Hunter, *Shakespeare and the Comedy of Forgiveness* (New York: Columbia UP, 1965), pp. 104–105.

3. George Brandes emphasizes the power of the play's realism: "If ever man was unworthy a woman's love, that man is Claudio. If ever marriage was odious and ill-omened, this is it" (quoted in John Russell Brown, *Shakespeare:* Much Ado about Nothing *and* As You Like It [London: Macmillan, 1979], p. 42). Leo Salingar, in *Shakespeare and the Traditions of Comedy* (Cambridge: Cambridge UP, 1974), touches upon this matter when he discusses *Much Ado* along with *The Merchant of Venice, All's Well That Ends Well,* and *Measure for Measure* in terms of their common source in Italian *novelle*. He finds all four plays exhibiting a central interest in the combination of "broken nuptials and a legal crisis" (305).

4. Paul and Miriam Mueschke, "Illusion and Metamorphosis in *Much Ado about Nothing,*" *Shakespeare Quarterly* 18 (1967): 65.

5. Arden, p. 90; Riverside, p. 332. Again and again, we see that *Much Ado* is the most communal of Shakespeare's comedies. No one is threatened, isolated, in danger until the plot against Hero unfolds. But it should be noted too that the comic community of the play is made up of people who are idle and in search of amusement.

6. This stage direction is supplied in the Arden edition. Although it has no textual authority, appearing neither in Q nor in F, it does describe the scene accurately.

7. See Ejner J. Jensen, "Spying Scenes and the Problem Plays: A Shakespearean Strategy," *Tulane Studies in English* 20 (1972): 33.

8. Jorg Häsler has a useful account of these scenes in *Shakespeare's Theatrical Notation: The Comedies*, The Cooper Monographs, Theatrical Physiognomy Series 21 (Bern: Francke Verlag, 1974), pp. 115–23. For a view of these scenes quite different from the one I advance here, see Carol Thomas Neely, *Broken Nuptials in Shakespeare's Plays* (New Haven: Yale UP, 1985), pp. 47–49.

9. Here again, a director has a choice. Is Benedick referring to Claudio, and is Claudio truly moved by the air Balthazar plays, or is he already in character for Don Pedro's little drama of deception? My own view, I think, will be clear from what follows.

10. This view of the function of the song (and of the parallelism of the scenes) is hardly new. H. H. Furness, in the 1899 Variorum Edition, quotes W. W. Lloyd, *Critical Essays*, Singer's Second Edition (London, 1856):

> The song of Balthazar is interposed not without purpose; . . . the burden of his song, encouraging ladies to sigh no more, is that of the ensuing conversation on the desirableness of Beatrice suppressing her passion. Benedick's preference for wind music is also a point of nature, and his sudden change of attitude, from that of a wearied overhearer of sentiment that bores him, to an anxious listener, when his proper affections are in question, is laughable enough; but the introduction of music has also the effect of supplying an intermediate tone of association, that softens the transition that we witness from one declared condition of feelings to another. In the corresponding scene of the deception of Beatrice, the

effect is achieved by another artifice, by the sweetness and flow of the versification in which Hero and Ursula hold their discourse.

(116)

11. Humphreys, "Introduction" to the Arden edition, p. 34.

12. See Jorg Häsler for a very different view of this closing scene, emphasizing the Friar's effort to bring things to a close, pp. 134–38.

13. Examples from the romances include the following uses of the word:

Paulina: I like your silence, it the more shows off
Your wonder.

(5.3.21–22)

Miranda: O wonder!
How many goodly creatures are there here!
How beauteous mankind is! O brave new world
That has such people in't!

(5.1.181–84)

Posthumus: Nay, do not wonder at it; you are made
Rather to wonder at the things you hear
Than to work any.

(5.3.53–55)

Gower: Marina . . .
. . . who hath gain'd
Of education all the grace
Which makes [her] both th' [heart] and place
Of general wonder.

(4 Ch. 5–11)

14. John Crick, "Messina," *Twentieth-Century Interpretations of* Much Ado about Nothing, ed. Walter R. Davis (Englewood Cliffs, N.J.: Prentice-Hall, 1969), p. 37. Originally published as "Much Ado about Nothing," *The Use of English* 17 (London: Chatto and Windus, 1964), pp. 223–27. In Davis, pp. 33–38.

15. Some of the more specialized approaches to the comedies may, of course, find *Much Ado* particularly well suited to analysis. Edward Berry, in *Shakespeare's Comic Rites* (Cambridge: Cambridge UP, 1984), makes good use of his emphasis on rites of initiation in his discussion of the play. See also Robert Grams Hunter, *Shakespeare and the Comedy of Forgiveness* (New York: Columbia UP, 1965); Joseph Westlund, *Shakespeare's Reparative Comedies: A Psychoanalytic View of the Middle Plays* (Chicago: U of Chicago P, 1984); and Marilyn Williamson, *The Patriarchy of Shakespeare's Comedies* (Detroit: Wayne State UP, 1986).

16. Prouty, *The Sources of* Much Ado about Nothing (New Haven: Yale UP, 1950), p. 61.

17. *The Riverside Shakespeare*, p. 327.

18. Joseph A. Bryant, Jr., *Shakespeare and the Uses of Comedy* (Lexington: UP of Kentucky, 1986), p. 126.

19. M. M. Mahood, "Shakespeare's Middle Comedies: A Generation of Criticism," *Shakespeare Survey* 32 (1979): 11.

20. A. P. Rossiter, "*Much Ado about Nothing*," *Angel with Horns and Other Shakespeare Lectures*, ed. Graham Story (London: Longmans, 1961), p. 80.

Four. Performative Comedy in *As You Like It*

1. William Shakespeare, *As You Like It*, The Arden Shakespeare, ed. Agnes Latham (London: Methuen, 1975), p. 126n.

2. Ruth Nevo, *Comic Transformations in Shakespeare* (London: Methuen, 1980), p. 196.

3. Charles H. Frey, *Experiencing Shakespeare: Essays on Text, Classroom, and Performance* (Columbia: U of Missouri P, 1988), p. 26.

4. Anthony B. Dawson, *Indirections: Shakespeare and the Art of Illusion* (Toronto: U of Toronto P, 1978), pp. vii, 37.

5. G. K. Hunter, *Shakespeare: The Later Comedies*, Writers and Their Works 143 (London: Longmans, Green, 1964), p. 41.

6. Harold Toliver, *Pastoral Forms and Attitudes* (Berkeley and Los Angeles: U of California P, 1971), p. 111.

7. R. Chris Hassel, *Faith and Folly in Shakespeare's Romantic Comedies* (Athens: U of Georgia P, 1980), pp. 22–23.

8. Jean E. Howard, in her review of "Recent Studies in Elizabethan and Jacobean Drama" (*Studies in English Literature* 27 [1987]: 321–79), makes the case against readings that are neither "theoretically addressed nor historically situated" (340). Commenting on a book she approves of (Richard A. Levin's *Love and Society in Shakespearean Comedy*), she nevertheless finds that it "invites in a special way reflection on the status of interpretation, especially on the political and historical determinants of those acts of textual production/reproduction we call readings" (340). She stops short of announcing the death of "the reading" as a critical activity.

9. Peter Erickson, *Patriarchal Structures in Shakespeare's Drama* (Berkeley and Los Angeles: U of California P, 1985).

10. The passages here, quoted from Mrs. Jameson, Gervinus, Shaw, Peter Phialas, and Hugh Richmond, are taken from the New Variorum Edition of *As You Like It*, ed. Richard Knowles, with a survey of criticism by Evelyn Joseph Mattern (New York: Modern Language Association of America, 1977), pp. 572–81. Charles Forker emphasizes the performative dimensions of Rosalind's role, stressing matters that differ from but complement my own emphasis on the character: "We watch her playing a theatrical game that combines pretense with sincerity, that involves both detachment and engagement at the same time, that mediates between an acerbic, intelligent wittiness and the pathos of longing." See "All the World's a Stage: Multiple Perspectives in Arden," *Iowa State Journal of Research* 54 (1980): 428.

11. Richard L. Levin, "Feminist Thematics and Shakespearean Tragedy," *PMLA* 103 (1988): 125–38.

12. Adrian Louis Montrose, " 'The Place of a Brother' in *As You Like It*: Social Process and Comic Form," *Shakespeare Quarterly* 32 (1981): 28–54.

13. Marilyn Williamson, *The Patriarchy of Shakespeare's Comedies* (Detroit: Wayne State UP, 1986), p. 45. See also Barbara J. Bono, "Mixed Gender, Mixed Genre in *As You Like It*," *Renaissance Genres: Essays on Theory, History, and Interpretation*, ed. Barbara Kiefer Lewalski, Harvard English Studies 14 (Cambridge: Harvard UP, 1986), pp. 189–212; and Phyllis Rackin, "An-

drogyny, Mimesis, and the Marriage of the Boy Heroine on the English Renaissance Stage," *PMLA* 102 (1987): 29–41.

14. David Young, *The Heart's Forest* (New Haven: Yale UP, 1972), p. 71.

15. Harold Jenkins, *"As You Like It," Shakespeare Survey* 8 (1955): 40–51; reprinted in *Twentieth-Century Interpretations of* As You Like It, ed. Jay Halio (Englewood Cliffs, N.J.: Prentice Hall, 1968), pp. 28, 29.

16. See Knowles, New Variorum, which I have used as the source of these headings from *Rosalynde*.

17. Michael R. Best, "Lyly's Static Drama," *Renaissance Drama* N.S. 1 (1968): 75–86.

18. See Young, p. 64.

19. "He was a bachelor then" (1.2.29) gives rise to a different sort of question when actresses key on the line as the opening of Viola's love interest in Orsino.

20. I recall a particularly leaden few minutes in the National Theatre production of 1979, directed by John Dexter. Sara Kestelman and Marjorie Yates, in elaborate Elizabethan dress, had little success in either filling the vast stage or interesting the audience.

21. This note is quoted from the text in *The Riverside Shakespeare*.

22. John Russell Brown, *Shakespeare and His Comedies*, 2nd ed. (London: Methuen, 1962, repr. 1973), p. 19.

23. What that honor signifies should be judged in the context of Touchstone's remarks at 1.2.75–82, where Frederick's love of the knight lacking honor associates him with the same deficiency.

24. "Content" is the key value of pastoral.

25. Comic preparation of this sort is a staple feature of Shakespeare's stagecraft; see my discussion of the technique in chapters 2 and 3.

26. Our memory of Silvius's earlier exit is likely to make the performative aspect of this action even more emphatic. For a complementary view of some performance elements in *As You Like It* see D. J. Palmer, "*As You Like It* and the Idea of Play," *Critical Quarterly* 13 (1971): 234–45.

Five. Speaking Masterly

1. John Russell Brown, "The Interpretation of Shakespeare's *Comedies*: 1900–1953," *Shakespeare Survey* 8 (1955): 1–13.

2. Alexander Leggatt, *Shakespeare's Comedy of Love* (London: Methuen, 1974), p. 223.

3. Bertrand Evans, of course, finds this the key to Shakespeare's comedies.

4. Ben Jonson, *The Alchemist*, ed. F. H. Mares, The Revels Plays (London: Methuen, 1967), 1.4.18–29.

5. F. H. Mares, "Introduction," *The Alchemist*, The Revels Plays (London: Methuen, 1967), p. 123. Actually, Mammon first sees Doll when she appears briefly, and Face describes her as the mad sister of a lord (2.3.210).

6. In the 1969 Stratford Festival production of the play, William Hutt provided a wonderful target for parody, especially in his distinctive walk.

7. William Shakespeare, *Twelfth Night*, The New Cambridge Shake-

speare, ed. Elizabeth Story Donno (Cambridge and New York: Cambridge UP, 1985), 1.1.18, 20, 32.

8. This is literally the case. Olivia seems curiously inattentive to her vow. Only when Viola approaches, halfway through the scene, does she call for her veil.

9. The Russian film version of *Twelfth Night,* though frequently off base, is right in this. It shows Orsino and Viola as already having achieved a physical closeness in 2.4. As Orsino leans against a tree, Viola listens adoringly to his talk, her elbow on his knee (Jack J. Jorgens, *Shakespeare on Film,* Bloomington: Indiana UP, 1977, p. 25).

10. See Leo Salingar's account of the play's structure, which argues for a division of the whole play along similar lines. "The Design of *Twelfth Night,*" Twelfth Night: *Critical Essays,* ed. Stanley Wells (New York: Garland, 1986), 191–225.

11. Clifford Leech, Twelfth Night *and Shakespearean Comedy* (Toronto: Dalhousie UP, 1965), p. 45.

12. See the account by Elizabeth Story Donno in which she traces three different ways of presenting Malvolio: straight, tragic, and burlesqued, in "Introduction," *Twelfth Night,* The New Cambridge Shakespeare (Cambridge and New York: Cambridge UP, 1985), p. 33.

13. This comment comes from a description by Philip Brockbank of the 1958–60 RSC production of the play, part of his contribution on "Recent Years" to the stage history provided in the New Cambridge edition (34).

Six. Comic Vitality and the Cost of Fantasy in *Measure for Measure*

1. See John Russell Brown, "The Interpretation of Shakespeare's Comedies: 1900-1953," *Shakespeare Survey* 8 (1955): 1–13.

2. Northrop Frye, *The Myth of Deliverance: Reflections on Shakespeare's Problem Comedies* (Toronto: U of Toronto P, 1983), p. 61.

3. Joan Rees, *Shakespeare and the Story: Aspects of Creation* (London: Athlone, 1978), p. 4; Harriet Hawkins, *Measure for Measure,* Harvester New Critical Introductions to Shakespeare (Brighton: The Harvester P, 1987), p. 38.

4. "Most criticism" would not include certain recent approaches, deconstructionist and others, whose first principles reject order and design.

5. This fault has been analyzed tellingly by Richard L. Levin. See his discussion of critical approaches to *Measure for Measure* in *New Readings vs. Old Plays: Recent Trends in the Reinterpretation of English Renaissance Drama* (Chicago: U of Chicago P, 1979), pp. 209-29.

6. Critical pressure seems especially intense in the work of critics who offer theological readings of the play. See the thoughtful and (I believe) persuasive reservations about such approaches in David Lloyd Stevenson, *The Achievement of Shakespeare's* Measure for Measure (Ithaca: Cornell UP, 1966), pp. 93-120.

7. Sir Arthur Quiller-Couch, "Introduction," *Measure for Measure,* The New Cambridge Edition (Cambridge: Cambridge UP, 1922), p. xxx; R. W. Chambers, *The Jacobean Shakespeare and* Measure for Measure (London: H. Milford, 1938), Annual British Academy Shakespeare Lecture, 1937, p. 40.

8. Rosalind Miles, *The Problem of* Measure for Measure: *A Historical Investigation* (New York: Barnes and Noble, 1976), pp. 216-17.

9. Bertrand Evans, *Shakespeare's Comedies* (Oxford: Oxford UP, 1960), p. 196; J. W. Lever, "Introduction," *Measure for Measure*, The Arden Shakespeare (London: Methuen, 1965), p. lxxvi.

10. See Bernice W. Kliman, "Isabella in *Measure for Measure*," *Shakespeare Studies* 15 (1982): 138-39. Kliman focuses on Isabella's rhetorical ineptitude in the play, but her reading of these opening lines essentially supports my view.

11. *Coleridge's Shakespearean Criticism*, ed. T. M. Raysor, 2 vols. (London: Constable, 1930), vol. 1, pp. 113–14.

12. See my comments on this convention in Ejner J. Jensen, "The Boy Actors: Plays and Playing," *Research Opportunities in Renaissance Drama* 18 (1975): 5–11.

13. Hawkins provides a catalogue of such efforts on pp. 102-10.

14. Theodore Spencer, *Shakespeare and the Nature of Man* (New York: Macmillan, 1942).

15. Bernard Beckerman, *Shakespeare at the Globe* (New York: Columbia UP, 1962), p. 39.

16. The same sort of discord appears in 2.2, where Lucio enters with Isabella on the Provost's "Save your honor" (25).

17. I part company with Anne Barton in her Riverside introduction, preferring to see the First Gentleman's remark not as a salutation to Mistress Overdone but as a response to Lucio. See J. W. Lever's note to 1.1.54-55 in the Arden edition.

18. Others have made the point. See Lever's note to 1.1.172–76 in the Arden edition.

19. Bertrand Evans comments on this extensively, though with a special emphasis on his central critical notion of "discrepant awareness," in *Shakespeare's Comedies*; but most critics of the play see this as a central feature of the play.

20. Hereward T. Price, *Construction in Shakespeare*, University of Michigan Contributions in Modern Philology 17 (Ann Arbor: U of Michigan P, 1951).

21. That Elbow returns later, still in office, has no bearing on this point. Apart from the fact that the play's time scheme does not allow his replacement, his return serves only to reinforce the pattern seen in 2.1.

22. The story is included in *The Viking Portable Dorothy Parker* (New York: Viking, 1944). See p. 60.

23. Alvin Kernan, in *The Cankered Muse: Satire of the English Renaissance* (New Haven: Yale UP, 1959), writes persuasively about the open-endedness of the satiric form, especially in comedy.

Works Cited

Barber, C. L. *Shakespeare's Festive Comedy: A Study of Dramatic Form and Its Relation to Social Custom.* 1959. Princeton: Princeton UP, 1972.

Barton, Anne. "*As You Like It* and *Twelfth Night*: Shakespeare's Sense of an Ending." *Shakespearian Comedy.* Stratford-upon-Avon Studies 14. Ed. Malcolm Bradbury and David Palmer. London: Edward Arnold, 1972.

———. "Shakespeare's Sense of an Ending in *Twelfth Night.*" Twelfth Night: *Critical Essays.* Ed. Stanley Wells. New York: Garland, 1986. 303–10.

Beckerman, Bernard. *Shakespeare at the Globe.* New York: Columbia UP, 1962.

Berry, Edward. *Shakespeare's Comic Rites.* Cambridge: Cambridge UP, 1984.

Berry, Ralph. *Shakespeare's Comedies: Explorations in Form.* Princeton: Princeton UP, 1972.

Best, Michael R. "Lyly's Static Drama." *Renaissance Drama* N.S. 1 (1968): 75–86.

Bonazza, Blaze. *Shakespeare's Early Comedies: A Structural Analysis.* Studies in English Literature 9. The Hague: Mouton, 1966.

Bono, Barbara J. "Mixed Gender, Mixed Genre in *As You Like It.*" *Renaissance Genres: Essays on Theory, History, and Interpretation.* Ed. Barbara Kiefer Lewalski. Harvard English Studies 14. Cambridge: Harvard UP, 1986. 189–212.

Brown, John Russell. "The Interpretation of Shakespeare's Comedies: 1900–1953." *Shakespeare Survey* 8 (1955): 1–13.

———. *Shakespeare's Dramatic Style*: Romeo and Juliet, As You Like It, Julius Caesar, Twelfth Night, Macbeth. London: Heinemann, 1970.

———. *Shakespeare and His Comedies.* 2nd ed. London: Methuen, 1962, 1973.

———. *Shakespeare:* Much Ado about Nothing *and* As You Like It. London: Macmillan, 1979.

Bryant, Joseph A., Jr. *Shakespeare and the Uses of Comedy.* Lexington: UP of Kentucky, 1986.

Carroll, D. Allen, and Gary J. Williams, eds. A Midsummer Night's Dream: *An Annotated Bibliography.* New York: Garland, 1986.

Carroll, William C. *The Metamorphoses of Shakespearean Comedy.* Princeton: Princeton UP, 1985.

Chambers, R. W. *The Jacobean Shakespeare and* Measure for Measure. London: H. Milford, 1938. Annual British Academy Shakespeare Lecture, 1937.

Coghill, Nevill. "The Basis of Shakespearean Comedy." *Essays and Studies* 3 (1950): 1–28.

Crick, John. "Messina." *Twentieth-Century Interpretations of* Much Ado about Nothing. Ed. Walter R. Davis. Englewood Cliffs, N.J.: Prentice-Hall, 1969. 33–38.

Danson, Lawrence. *The Harmonies of* The Merchant of Venice. New Haven: Yale UP, 1978.
Davis, Walter R., ed. *Twentieth-Century Interpretations of* Much Ado about Nothing. Englewood Cliffs, N.J.: Prentice-Hall, 1969.
Dawson, Anthony B. *Indirections: Shakespeare and the Art of Illusion*. Toronto: U of Toronto P, 1978.
Edwards, Philip. *Shakespeare and the Confines of Art*. London: Methuen, 1968.
Erickson, Peter. *Patriarchal Structures in Shakespeare's Drama*. Berkeley and Los Angeles: U of California P, 1985.
Evans, Bertrand. *Shakespeare's Comedies*. Oxford: Oxford UP, 1960.
Evans, G. Blakemore, et al., eds. *The Riverside Shakespeare*. Boston: Houghton Mifflin, 1974.
Fender, Stephen. *Shakespeare:* A Midsummer Night's Dream. London: Edward Arnold, 1968.
Forker, Charles. "All the World's a Stage: Multiple Perspectives in Arden." *Iowa State Journal of Research* 54 (1980): 421–30.
Frey, Charles H. *Experiencing Shakespeare: Essays on Text, Classroom, and Performance*. Columbia: U of Missouri P, 1988.
Frye, Northrop. *The Anatomy of Criticism: Four Essays*. Princeton: Princeton UP, 1957.
———. "The Argument of Comedy." *English Institute Essays 1948*. Ed. D. A. Robertson, Jr. New York: Columbia UP, 1949. 58–73.
———. *The Myth of Deliverance: Reflections on Shakespeare's Problem Comedies*. Toronto: U of Toronto P, 1983.
———. *A Natural Perspective: The Development of Shakespearean Comedy and Romance*. New York: Columbia UP, 1965.
Greene, Robert. *Friar Bacon and Friar Bungay*. Ed. Daniel Seltzer. Regents Renaissance Drama Series. Lincoln: U of Nebraska P, 1963.
Häsler, Jorg. *Shakespeare's Theatrical Notation: The Comedies*. The Cooper Monographs. Theatrical Physiognomy Series 21. Bern: Francke Verlag, 1974.
Hassel, R. Chris. *Faith and Folly in Shakespeare's Romantic Comedies*. Athens: U of Georgia P, 1980.
Hawkins, Harriet. *Measure for Measure*. Harvester New Critical Introductions to Shakespeare. Brighton: The Harvester P, 1987.
Howard, Jean E. "Recent Studies in Elizabethan and Jacobean Drama." *Studies in English Literature* 27 (1987): 321–79.
Hunter, G. K. *Shakespeare: The Later Comedies*. Writers and Their Works 143. London: Longmans, Green, 1964.
Hunter, Robert Grams. *Shakespeare and the Comedy of Forgiveness*. New York: Columbia UP, 1965.
Jagendorf, Zvi. *The Happy End of Comedy: Jonson, Molière, and Shakespeare*. Newark: U of Delaware P, 1984.
Jenkins, Harold. *"As You Like It." Shakespeare Survey* 8 (1955): 40–51. Reprinted in *Twentieth-Century Interpretations of* As You Like It. Ed. Jay Halio. Englewood Cliffs, N.J.: Prentice-Hall, 1968. 28–43.
Jensen, Ejner J. "The Boy Actors: Plays and Playing." *Research Opportunities in Renaissance Drama* 18 (1975): 5–11.

———. "Spying Scenes and the Problem Plays: A Shakespearean Strategy." *Tulane Studies in English* 20 (1972): 23–40.

Johnson, Samuel. "Preface to Shakespeare." *Johnson on Shakespeare.* Ed. Arthur Sherbo. Vol. 7, the Yale Edition of the Works of Samuel Johnson. 14 vols. Ed. E. L. McAdam, Jr., et al. New Haven: Yale UP, 1968.

Jonson, Ben. *The Alchemist.* Ed. F. H. Mares. The Revels Plays. London: Methuen, 1967.

———. *Epicoene, or, The Silent Woman.* Ed. L. A. Beaurline. Regents Renaissance Drama Series. Lincoln: U of Nebraska P, 1966.

———. *Volpone, or, The Fox.* Ed. R. B. Parker. The Revels Plays. Manchester: Manchester UP, 1983.

Jorgens, Jack J. *Shakespeare on Film.* Bloomington: Indiana UP, 1977.

Kermode, Frank. "The Mature Comedies." *Early Shakespeare.* Stratford-upon-Avon-Studies 3. Ed. John Russell Brown and Bernard Harris. London: Edward Arnold, 1961.

———. *The Sense of an Ending.* New York: Oxford UP, 1967.

Kernan, Alvin. *The Cankered Muse: Satire of the English Renaissance.* New Haven: Yale UP, 1959.

———. *The Plot of Satire.* New Haven: Yale UP, 1965.

Kliman, Bernice. "Isabella in *Measure for Measure.*" *Shakespeare Studies* 15 (1982): 137–48.

Kott, Jan. *Shakespeare Our Contemporary.* Trans. Boleslaw Taborski. 2nd ed. London: Methuen, 1967.

Krieger, Elliot. *A Marxist Study of Shakespeare's Comedies.* Totowa, N.J.: Barnes and Noble, 1979.

Kyd, Thomas. *The Spanish Tragedy.* Ed. Philip Edwards. The Revels Plays. Cambridge: Harvard UP, 1959.

Leech, Clifford. Twelfth Night *and Shakespearean Comedy.* Toronto: Dalhousie UP, 1965.

Leggatt, Alexander. *Shakespeare's Comedy of Love.* London: Methuen, 1974.

Levin, Richard A. *Love and Society in Shakespearean Comedy.* Newark: U of Delaware P, 1985.

Levin, Richard L. *New Readings vs. Old Plays: Recent Trends in the Reinterpretation of English Renaissance Drama.* Chicago: U of Chicago P, 1979.

———. "Feminist Thematics and Shakespearean Tragedy." *PMLA* 103 (1988): 125–38.

Lyons, Charles R. *Shakespeare and the Ambiguity of Love's Triumph.* Studies in English Literature 68. The Hague: Mouton, 1971.

MacCary, Thomas. *Friends and Lovers: The Phenomenology of Desire in Shakespearean Comedy.* New York: Columbia UP, 1985.

Mahood, M. M. "Shakespeare's Middle Comedies: A Generation of Criticism." *Shakespeare Survey* 32 (1979): 1–13.

Miles, Rosalind. *The Problem of* Measure for Measure: *A Historical Investigation.* New York: Barnes and Noble, 1976.

Montrose, Adrian Louis. " 'The Place of a Brother' in *As You Like It*: Social Process and Comic Form." *Shakespeare Quarterly* 32 (1981): 28–54.

Moody, A. D. *Shakespeare:* The Merchant of Venice. London: Edward Arnold, 1964.

Mueschke, Paul, and Miriam Mueschke. "Illusion and Metamorphosis in *Much Ado about Nothing*." *Shakespeare Quarterly* 18 (1967): 53–65.

Neely, Carol Thomas. *Broken Nuptials in Shakespeare's Plays*. New Haven: Yale UP, 1985. 47–49.

Nevo, Ruth. *Comic Transformations in Shakespeare*. London: Methuen, 1980.

Palmer, D. J. "*As You Like It* and the Idea of Play." *Critical Quarterly* 13 (1971): 234–45.

Parker, Dorothy. *The Viking Portable Dorothy Parker*. New York: Viking, 1944.

Price, Hereward T. *Construction in Shakespeare*. University of Michigan Contributions in Modern Philology. Ann Arbor: U of Michigan P, 1951.

______. "Mirror Scenes in Shakespeare." *Joseph Quincy Adams Memorial Studies*. Ed. James G. McManaway et al. Washington, D.C.: The Folger Shakespeare Library, 1948. 101–13.

Prouty, Charles T. *The Sources of* Much Ado about Nothing. New Haven: Yale UP, 1950.

Rabkin, Norman. *Shakespeare and the Problem of Meaning*. Chicago: U of Chicago P, 1981.

Rackin, Phyllis. "Androgyny, Mimesis, and the Marriage of the Boy Heroine on the English Renaissance Stage." *PMLA* 102 (1987): 29–41.

Raysor, T. M. *Coleridge's Shakespearean Criticism*. 2 vols. London: Constable, 1930.

Rebhorn, Wayne A. "After Frye: A Review-Article on the Interpretation of Shakespearean Comedy and Romance." *Texas Studies in Language and Literature* 21 (1979): 553–82.

Rees, Joan. *Shakespeare and the Story: Aspects of Creation*. London: Athlone, 1978.

Riemer, A. P. *Antic Fables: Patterns of Evasion in Shakespeare's Comedies*. New York: St. Martins, 1980.

Rossiter, A. P. "*Much Ado about Nothing*." *Angel with Horns and Other Shakespearean Lectures*. Ed. Graham Story. London: Longmans, 1961. 65–81.

Salingar, Leo. "The Design of *Twelfth Night*." Twelfth Night: *Critical Essays*. Ed. Stanley Wells. New York: Garland, 1986. 191–225.

______. *Shakespeare and the Traditions of Comedy*. Cambridge: Cambridge UP, 1974.

Shackford, John B. "The Bond of Kindness: Shylock's Humility." *University of Kansas City Review*, Winter 1954: 85–91.

Shakespeare, William. *As You Like It*. New Variorum Edition. Ed. Richard Knowles. New York: Modern Language Association of America, 1977.

______. *As You Like It*. The Arden Shakespeare. Ed. Agnes Latham. London: Methuen, 1975.

______. *Measure for Measure*. The Arden Shakespeare. Ed. J. W. Lever. London: Methuen, 1965.

______. *Measure for Measure*. The New Cambridge Edition. Ed. Sir Arthur Quiller-Couch. Cambridge: Cambridge UP, 1922.

______. *The Merchant of Venice*. The Arden Shakespeare. Ed. John Russell Brown. London: Methuen, 1955.

———. *Much Ado about Nothing*. New Variorum Edition. Ed. H. H. Furness. Philadelphia, 1899.

———. *Much Ado about Nothing*. The Arden Shakespeare. Ed. A. R. Humphreys. London: Methuen, 1981.

———. *The Riverside Shakespeare*. Ed. G. Blakemore Evans. Boston: Houghton Mifflin, 1974.

———. *Twelfth Night*. The New Cambridge Shakespeare. Ed. Elizabeth Story Donno. Cambridge and New York: Cambridge UP, 1985.

Shapiro, James. "'Which Is *The Merchant* Here, and Which *The Jew*?': Shakespeare and the Economics of Influence." *Shakespeare Studies* 20 (1988): 269–79.

Smith, Barbara Herrnstein. *Poetic Closure: A Study of How Poems End*. Chicago: U of Chicago P, 1968.

Spencer, Theodore. *Shakespeare and the Nature of Man*. New York: Macmillan, 1942.

Stevenson, David Lloyd. *The Achievement of Shakespeare's* Measure for Measure. Ithaca: Cornell UP, 1966.

Styan, J. L. *Shakespeare's Stagecraft*. Cambridge: Cambridge UP, 1967.

Summers, Joseph. "The Masks of *Twelfth Night*." *University of Kansas City Review* 22 (1955): 25–32.

Swindon, Patrick. *An Introduction to Shakespeare's Comedies*. London: Macmillan, 1973.

Toliver, Harold. *Pastoral Forms and Attitudes*. Berkeley and Los Angeles: U of California P, 1971.

Van Laan, Thomas. *Role-Playing in Shakespeare*. Toronto: U of Toronto P, 1978.

Westlund, Joseph. *Shakespeare's Reparative Comedies: A Psychoanalytic View of the Middle Plays*. Chicago: U of Chicago P, 1984.

White, R. S. *Shakespeare and the Romance Ending*. Newcastle: Tyneside Free P, 1981.

Williamson, Marilyn. *The Patriarchy of Shakespeare's Comedies*. Detroit: Wayne State UP, 1986.

Wilson, John Dover. *Shakespeare's Happy Comedies*. London: Faber and Faber, 1962.

Young, David. *The Heart's Forest*. New Haven: Yale UP, 1972.

———. *Something of Great Constancy: The Art of* A Midsummer Night's Dream. New Haven: Yale UP, 1966.

Index

EJNER J. JENSEN is Professor of English Language and Literature at the University of Michigan, where he has taught since 1964. The author of studies of John Marston and Ben Jonson, he has also published articles and essays on topics ranging from Renaissance drama, satire, and theatre history to W. B. Yeats, Richard Wilbur, and Shakespeare's presence in modern poetry. In addition, he is the editor of a collection of essays entitled *The Future of* "Nineteen Eighty-Four."